FINANCING ADULT
EDUCATION AND TRAINING

KEITH DRAKE

MANCHESTER
MONOGRAPHS
21

June 1983

ISBN 0 903717 31 X

Printed by: Direct Design (Bournemouth) Ltd., Printers,
Butts Pond Industrial Estate, Sturminster Newton, Dorset DT10 1AZ

CONTENTS

LIST OF TABLES

LIST OF FIGURES

PREFACE

The economics of the financing of adult education and training, which is too cumbersome as a title, is the real theme of these five essays. Existing knowledge and concepts from economics are brought to bear on aspects of the financing and resourcing of adult learning. The focus is not that of accountancy: cash transactions and money outlays. The focus is on consequences. How do financing arrangements influence the commitment and use of all scarce resources in aid of learning by adults? How do these arrangements affect who learns what, when, where and how? These are very large questions. Very often nobody knows the answers. All that is attempted here is a consideration of some pointers which are available in work done by other people over the twenty years since the publication of Roby Kidd's Financing Continuing Education (1962).

These essays are exploratory. They start from the position that it may be an advantage to dispense with some of the standard but implicit assumptions of so much policy analysis: that value can be equated with market price; that learning is a direct function of teaching; that more public spending will increase the availability of educational resources to adult learners; that formal is 'better' than non-formal education. Financing arrangements should be judged primarily in terms of their influence on the way in which scarce resources are allocated and managed in pursuit of major goals like personal development, cultural enrichment, social justice and increased productivity. To do this is very difficult; and sometimes the result is not unfairly characterised as trying to make bricks without straw. However, policy analysis needs to become more relevant to the realities of adult learning amid the fierce competition for resources in developed countries. It may be useful to abandon certain convenient assumptions and familiar modes of analysis and to cast some half-baked bread upon the waters.

My debt to the work and thinking of others is indicated in the extensive list of references. I am also grateful to generous friends and colleagues, in England and abroad. Over many years they have, with patience and kindness, helped me to cut back on error and illogicality. The mistakes, obscurities and values in this text are all my own responsibility.

Keith Drake
Manchester, November, 1982.

CHAPTER ONE :   SOME FUNDAMENTALS

ANALYSIS :   SELECTING THE CORRECT MODEL

Interest in the financing of adult education often arises out of a desire
to control the provision of learning opportunities for adults. To some
people, both learners and non-learners, learning is valuable. To
others that same learning may be a threat or a danger. Anyway it is
expensive: it will use up scarce resources which have other and competing uses. Because of these characteristics the control and, indeed,
rationing of learning opportunities is a major concern in all countries.

The most easily available public financial data are generally the by-
product of a concern with political accountability and good administra-
tion. Politicians, administrators, electors and taxpayers want to see
whether money voted for adult education has been spent as voted, and
only as voted, and whether it has been used efficiently to achieve
publicly-agreed goals. In many developed countries non-government
collective organisations like firms and voluntary associations play a
larger part than government in the financing of adult education. Here
too the emphasis is on control of opportunities in response to the objectives of those who wield power. This audit or stewardship approach to
financing is proper and important. But it is not the approach adopted in
this essay. Instead, the focus is on the financial dimension of policy
analysis.

Policy analysis is a matter of considering alternative actions, predicting
consequences and valuing outcomes. Choices are a matter for the
individual, the firm, the association or government. No analyst can
grasp the real world as these choosers experience it in all its rich
complexity. The job of the analyst is to discover, organise and make
accessible a mass of information relevant to choices. The result is a
simplified representation or model of the real world. Loss of realism
is an inevitable concomitant of analysis. This is worthwhile provided that
the loss of realism is outweighed by improved insight and manageability.

Some forms of policy analysis use a rational model, i.e. they impute to
the actors rationality in decision-making. Others use a semi-rational
model, in which this rational behaviour only obtains within defined limits;

or a non-rational model in which decisions are the product of incoherent social or political bargaining and of sheer accident. In the search for norms with which to evaluate and guide financing decisions it is to the rational and semi-rational models that analysts usually turn. A good model describes selected but important elements of an activity. It helps us to understand structural relationships and key tendencies. The quality of financial analysis depends in the first instance on the quality of the model being used. One of the best known rational models used in analysing corporate and individual decisions about training (Becker, 1975) makes the assumption that employers are trying to maximise profits. But alternative 'as if' models of the firm have also yielded useful conclusions concerning the behaviour of firms when financing training. The behaviour of firms may be analysed 'as if' they were seeking to maximise sales revenue or asset values, or not trying to maximise at all but to maintain an existing reputation as 'a good trainer' for industrial relations reasons. Indeed, some firms see themselves as a centre of excellence within an industry or region and effectively elevate being a good trainer into an independent company objective (see Oatey, 1970; Ryan, 1980).

One of the earliest decisions which has to be made in modelling or simplifying the real world is how to establish what information is relevant. For example, how should adult education be defined? In developed countries many professional educators and politicians have a bias towards formal education, even to the extent of equating formal education and education. If financial aid is to be given from tax funds, to help adults to learn, professional educators and politicians may prefer a highly visible and elaborate programme. But formal programmes are not necessarily the best way of achieving good results. Helene Hanff, author of 84 Charing Cross Road, tells how, as a young office worker, she cherished the ambition of becoming a playwright. The Theatre Guild decided that one way of helping would-be playwrights would be to finance promising young writers while they practised their craft. Two were selected, given $1,500 each, and told to go away and write. The following year, the Theatre Guild was persuaded that there was a better way to help people learn the business. It chose twelve people, including Helene Hanff, and provided an elaborate programme of seminars, visits to rehearsals and workshops. None of this dozen ever managed to write a commercial play. The two chosen the year before were Tennessee Williams and Arthur Miller.

It may be true that, in some sense, 'approximately half of the adult population in Britain has had no further education or training since

completing their initial education' (ACACE, 1982, p. 11). Fortunately,
adults do not depend entirely on formal education or training for learning opportunities, so this undoubtedly disadvantaged half of the adult
population has managed to learn a great deal even without the blessing
of 'further education and training'. It is not surprising that professional
adult educators are so concerned with formal provision, nor that
statisticians, for different reasons, prefer deliberately designed and
readily identifiable programmes rather than educational movements like
Do-It-Yourself. But the fundamental issue for educational policy is to
decide and implement public policy on the availability and distribution of
learning opportunities for adults, whether or not these occur in the
context of formal education. Unless there are good reasons to the
contrary, education for adults does not necessarily imply instructors or
teachers. At its broadest, the concept of education has to include what
is learned on the job in the sense of learning-by-doing and without the
assistance of recognizable instruction by someone else. It has to en-
compass private study by adults, whether this involves teaching oneself
joinery with the aid of library books, Handyman Which?, tools and wood;
or taking a London University external degree entirely by private study,
which is the demanding pastime of around 2,000 adults a year in Britain
(Sassoon, 1982, p. 10). It is an expository convenience to talk about
'adult education' as if it is a homogeneous substance like lard, with one
pound very much the same as any other. But it is frequently an analytical
trap to think of it in this way, because adult learning is various in form
and substance. Our attitude to who should bear the costs of providing
resources varies quite properly according to the nature of this learning
and who the learner is. Learning can often be resourced in more than
one way, and financing arrangements can influence the mode of
resourcing. So the nature and mode of adult learning must both be
specified in policy analysis.

A case can be made (e.g. Woodhall, 1980) for following UNESCO's
International Standard Classification of Education, which restricts adult
education to organised programmes for those aged fifteen and over not
in the regular school and university system. By contrast, the Education
Committee of OECD has chosen a much wider definition as being suitable
for policy-making :

> 'Adult Education refers to any learning activity or programme
> deliberately designed by a providing agent to satisfy any learning
> need or interest that may be experienced at any stage in his or
> her life by a person who is over the statutory school leaving age

and whose principal activity is no longer in education. Its
ambit, thus, spans non-vocational, vocational, general,
formal and non-formal studies as well as education with a
collective social purpose.

(OECD, 1977, p. 11)

This definition does not quite manage the commonsense equation of
adult education with the education of adults, since it still excludes those
adults whose principal activity is learning and whose initial education
has been terminated for whatever reason. It stops short of comprehend-
ing all post compulsory education, and equates best with continuing
education. However, the OECD definition includes not only organised
programmes of instruction but also non-formal education, where it may
be impossible to identify enrolled students. The data problems implicit
in the UNESCO definition are formidable. With the OECD definition these
problems become immense.

Perhaps the best way to resolve this difficulty is to adopt a double
standard. The difficulty arises from an essential problem of any modelling: the tension between manageability and realism. The UNESCO
definition is more manageable; the OECD definition is more realistic in
its recognition of the variety of adult learning, and could only usefully be
extended by including any structured learning occurring after the ending
of full-time initial education, whether or not this is a person's principal
activity. The double standard solution hinges on the appropriateness of
definition for purpose. It employs the distinction between the specific
and the general. Whenever the analysis of a specific educational activity
is in question, e.g. an adult literacy programme or retraining for unemployed workers, the definition should be appropriate to the purpose and
scope of the analysis. On the other hand, where the analysis is general,
e.g. concerned with the principles of public policy, a very comprehensive definition is usually better, accepting the penalty of great statistical
difficulties. If a very comprehensive definition is not used, the analyst
removes from consideration a vast and varied field of resource-
consuming learning opportunities which occur at work, at home or in the
community at large. A relatively narrow definition like that used in
ISCED has the disadvantage, in policy formation, that it produces a
dramatically unbalanced and grossly inaccurate picture of adult learning
opportunities. This almost invariably leads to neglect of very important
possibilities for substitution between learning in less formal and more
formal modes. Financial arrangements are rarely neutral in their effect
on choice of learning mode. So, when financial changes are made, one of

the consequences to be monitored is their effect on people's choice of setting within which to learn. One of the long-term trends observable in many developed countries is the formalisation of adult learning, the tendency to shift learning from workplace or home into an educational institution. Some of the latest developments in educational technology might appear to be reversing this shift. But formalisation is a powerful movement, in which financing arrangements play a major role, and it is not necessarily the most cost-effective way of promoting adult learning.

However, if this double standard definitional strategy is followed, it is essential to recognise openly the magnitude of margins of error and the immense gaps in the data. It may be more sensible to recognise them than to pretend that they do not exist, or that they exist but are not relevant to policy-making. It is necessary to quantify whatever can be quantified; and to indicate as clearly as possible what has not been incorporated into the quantification and the likely significance of these items. Uncertainty is very uncomfortable and inconvenient for the analyst; but it is no part of policy-making to make life easy for analysts. Concentration on the quantifiable soon leads analyst and client to identify the quantifiable with the important. Down this road lies sub-optimisation, a common disease of economics when used in policy analysis. Suboptimising, or trying to achieve the best for a part of a system (e.g. the quantifiable part), is not always best for the whole system. Indeed, Kenneth Boulding has gone as far as to argue that rationality about a sub-system can be worse than sub-rationality about the whole.

Adult learning is sometimes conceived as a dependence continuum. This continuum ranges from learning which is largely independent of any teacher, organised course or educational institution to learning which is heavily dependent on such aids. Two examples can be given of types of adult education which are quantitatively of massive importance but are only recorded in a marginal, fragmentary and often unrecognisable way by the data of formal education systems. Their existence points up the grave inadequacy of the definitions of adult education implicit in con-temporary data systems.

The first example relates to the mass of educational resources designed to assist genuinely private adult learning, not merely libraries and instructional programmes but a wealth of learning aids produced by the market sector or by voluntary bodies. Allen Tough's studies (1971 and 1978) of the average Canadian have produced an estimate that self-directed learning projects, of at least seven hours duration, account for about four out of every five identified learning projects. These self-directed projects are planned, carried through and monitored by adults outside formal educational settings. Tough has demonstrated both the variety of adult learning projects and the enormous significance of the time which adults devote to sustained, self-directed and highly deliberate efforts to learn. An activity which accounts for something of the order of 700 hours a year or 10 per cent of an adult's waking time deserves far more attention than it has received.

The second example concerns learning which is strictly related to paid work. Recent research in England and Wales (Killeen and Bird, 1981) suggests that just one, carefully defined form of this kind of adult education, paid educational leave, was experienced during 1976/77 by about one in six of all employees aged 19 years and over. These three or four million people underwent 25 to 30 million days of training, approximately 8 days per student, and only two fifths of this attendance took place in formal educational establishments in the conventional further and higher education sector of the British education system. Such research findings are fragmentary. Nevertheless, it is difficult to deny the accumulating evidence that in most OECD countries there is a very heavy commitment of adult time and of other scarce resources which takes many forms and is spread right along the dependence continuum (see OECD, 1977; Schuller and Megarry, 1979).

Since this is the nature of adult education in developed countries, financial issues are best considered in the context of a comprehensive public policy on the education of adults. Such a policy is still quite unknown in some countries, for instance the United Kingdom. The last major official report on adult education in England and Wales, the so-called Russell Report (1973), was confined by its terms of reference to something called 'non-vocational adult education' and to the fringes of provision in aid of adult learning. It is a mistake to define certain skills and knowledge as vocational or non-vocational, when it is the student's motive which may or may not be job-related (see ACACE, 1982, pp. 173-174). The error was not one which any committee could overcome. The committee was aware of the problem (Russell Report, 1973, p. 1), if not of the extent to which such an ill-founded restriction of the area of analysis vitiated the entire exercise. In October 1980 the Department of Education and Science demonstrated its continuing misunderstanding of the nature of adult education in a discussion paper on post-experience vocational provision for those in employment (DES, 1980). One of that

discussion paper's unsurprising features was an almost complete neglect
of existing and potential complimentarities and substitutions between
formal and non-formal continuing education, and between learning on the
job and off the job, combined with the Department's traditional neglect
of the important independent further education sector in the United
Kingdom. For the purposes of policy analysis or policy formation it is
necessary to employ a comprehensive notion of adult learning, and, at
bottom, a comprehensive analysis of society's resources for the production and distribution of knowledge (e. g. Machlup, 1962 and 1980).

It is possible to make too much of the lack of information about the
financing of adult education. Financial data are important, need to be
and could be greatly improved. But they are only a part, and sometimes a misleading part, of the data of choice. What is most lacking is
an adequately conceptualised and articulated framework of losses and
gains within which to set financial data.

By themselves financial data are not very illuminating. Frequently,
they measure only some of the input of resources in aid of adult learning.
Sometimes they include the cost of teacher time; often they ignore the
value of teacher time given voluntarily or by workers other than professional trainers or teachers. Frequently they undercost or ignore
entirely the value of learner time and also capital costs. What resources
they do measure they may not measure very accurately. Only rarely
are these partial and possibly inaccurate input measures related to
desired or achieved outcomes from adult education.

In order to assist learning, the household, the firm or government has
to renounce the benefits from other uses for scarce resources. This is
done in the expectation of beneficial outcomes, some pecuniary, some
non-pecuniary. In other words, one set and quantity of benefits is renounced in order to gain, through education, another set and quantity of
benefits. Some of the resources used are bought and have a recorded
financial cost. Some of the expected benefits are financial: they may
show up in increased sales or profits, or in education-related earnings
differentials. But purchased resources have to be related to unpurchased
resources; marketed outcomes have to be related to non-marketed outcomes. Normally, the purchase resources produce no learning except
in combination with unpurchased resources, and non-marketed outcomes
are unavoidably joint products with the marketed outcomes. So the
financial costs of an educational activity, and the financial benefits, can
only be meaningfully evaluated within the framework of all the renounced

benefits and <u>all</u> the expected benefits. These renounced benefits are what economists call the opportunity or economic costs of an activity, and they are often very different in magnitude and incidence from the financial costs. They are the value of benefits expected from the most-preferred alternative use of resources, a value which is foregone when resources are committed to a specified activity. This calculus, more comprehensive than a merely financial one, is used everyday, in practice, to allocated resources to an educational rather than a non-educational use, or to one kind of educational activity rather than another. It is used in the household, the firm, the voluntary association and in government. It is a (renounced) benefit: (expected) benefit analysis.

For instance, an adult may be choosing how to use leisure time, which is not the less valuable because it has not been priced in a labour market like time devoted to paid work. The renounced benefit, that which is foregone by devoting leisure hours to education, is a powerful choice-influencing cost which is frequently a major factor governing the response of individuals to course offerings and drop-out from courses. The adult will not opt for an educational use of time unless the benefits from it seem likely to exceed in value those which are being sacrificed. The renounced benefit is not costed in any market, signalled by any cash transaction, recorded in any ledger. It is evaluated by the potential adult learner, and may well influence the behaviour of that adult more than any money which would have to be spent on fares, tuition fees or books. Similarly, many outcomes are not sold to anyone, so market-generated financial measures are not available. Outcomes relating to equity or to the quality of life are not marketed. They may be revealed and even measurable, in certain ways, but not always in money terms.

It is to a comprehensive benefit: benefit analysis that policymakers have to turn in order to treat financial issues. Indeed, financial analysis will be profoundly misconstrued and will be misleading in its conse-quences unless it is recognised to be intimately related to and a subset of this benefit: benefit analysis. Many financial decisions have to be taken, for example

- how to raise money;
- what to spend it on;
- how much to spend;
- how much to charge in fees;
- how to channel tax funds to providers or to learners.

It is rarely appropriate to settle financial issues by using financial criteria alone. Such decisions need to be taken in the light of a clear and detailed account of all outcomes, whether these outcomes are costs (foregone benefits) or expected benefits. The budgetary implications of decisions are evaluated in the context of a comparison between a valuation of the next-best action and the benefits expected from the preferred action. Far more than expenditure implications are taken into account.

ANALYSIS: USEFUL DISTINCTIONS

In examining the financing of adult education it is helpful to employ some simple distinctions

- between internal and external efficiency;
- between efficiency and equity;
- between the positive and the normative.

External and internal efficiency

In this essay attention is focused on issues of external rather than internal efficiency. Internal efficiency concerns the private life of adult education, i.e. the teaching-learning process and the way in which human and material resources are combined to achieve human learning. Some ways of learning are more expensive of resources — less efficient — than others. Financial arrangements frequently govern the terms on which some of these resources are available and provide market valuations for some kinds of learning. They predispose people toward one particular way of managing learning, even if that is not the most efficient way of combining all committed resources. Minimising the cost of purchased resources devoted to marketed outputs may not minimise cost in terms of purchased plus unpurchased resources devoted to unmarketed as well as marketed outcomes.

But in this essay it is the consequences of financial arrangements for external efficiency which are considered. At the highest level of generality this external efficiency may be said to describe a relationship between education and the host society and economy. To assess external efficiency it is necessary to relate the outcomes of adult education to the social and economic objectives of the society or sub-group which provides the resources.

Efficiency and equity

In order to compare the effects which are desired (objectives) with
those which actually occur (outcomes) economists frequently classify
effects into

- consequences for economic growth: efficiency effects
- consequences for the distribution of income and of life chances :
equity effects (cf. Schultz, 1972; OECD, 1975)

A comprehensive study would have to investigate financing in terms of
each of the various concepts of efficiency and equity used by economists
(see Levin, 1976; Barlow, 1981; Le Grand, 1982). Moreover, application of any concept of efficiency involves a measurement and evaluation of outcomes, and that requires someone or some group of people to
make value judgements about private and collective benefits. There is
no such thing as a value-free efficiency measure. It is unfortunate that
economists use the same word, efficiency, in several different senses.
In the case of internal efficiency it describes a relationship between
inputs to and outputs from a process. In the case of external efficiency
it describes a relationship between outputs from a process and
externally-set objectives. When used in opposition to equity, efficiency
does not refer to a relationship of any kind. Instead, it acts as a
synonym for materialist and refers to a flow of goods and services.
Educating adults may well affect the pattern and volume of goods and
services which are produced. This is so when education is deliberately
contrived to do so — industrial training — and is clearly an investment
process. It is also true when it is conceived by learners or provided
as a simple consumption good — a means of satisfying our immediate
wants — because in the end it often influences our productivity in paid
or unpaid work.

These efficiency effects may be contrasted with the consequences of
adult education for the distribution of income between individuals at one
moment of time or over a lifetime. Education as investment or as consumption is liable to change the lifetime income profiles of adult
learners, whether these profiles are conceived narrowly as a stream of
annual money incomes or more fundamentally as lifetime consumption
profiles. Different kinds of adult education, experienced by different
groups of adults, produce different efficiency and equity effects.
Financing arrangements profoundly influence the distribution of many
resources in aid of adult learning. These arrangements largely control
who gets what, when and how, so one way of evaluating such arrangements is to relate them to observed efficiency and equity effects
(outcomes).

To conceptualise and to identify efficiency and equity effects is one task; to measure them is another matter. Economists have an understandable predeliction for additive measures, in fact, for monetisation. But this can undo the good work of separating out efficiency from equity outcomes by illegitimately collapsing them into one inscrutable value. The confusion of educational effects which are quite different in kind occurs in various ways. Often the process is rendered totally invisible by the administrative habit of treating spending on a programme — purchased resources plus any transfer payments — as a measure of output. Spending on a number of disparate programmes, which have different kinds of outcomes, is summed. Total spending is then treated as a meaningful valuation of adult learning achieved, even though separate outcomes by programme have been neither identified nor measured. Even then there is a tendency to lose many of the informational gains which might have been won. For example, a re-training scheme for unemployed adults can result in a reduction in financial costs to the taxpayer in the form of saved unemployment benefits. If unemployed adults are effectively lifted from unemployment into productive employment there is an equity gain, provided that other adults are not simply displaced in the labour market so that unemployment is reshuffled between individuals. There is also an efficiency gain in the form of increased overall productivity of the labour force, which can be more or less precisely quantified through the improved post-training incomes of trainees. The equity gain changes the distribution of incomes; the efficiency gain produces an increase in total real income. There are savings to the taxpayer, but it is illicit to add the value of these savings to the value of the increase in total real income in order to measure the total outcome from training. Savings to the taxpayer provide a convenient statistic indubitably tied to the extent of the programme and success of its employment objective. But they do not measure the value of the equity gain involved in altering the distribution of incomes as well as the employment status of adults. Nor can a transfer payment (saved) be added to a real gain in the form of the increased productivity of scarce resources.

It is also the case that efficiency and equity objectives can be competitive. The movement for recurrent education in the seventies arose out of a campaign against accelerating educational obsolescence among adults, and against formal education provision which had become excessively front-loaded, overblown and credential-bound. Recurrent education was a movement not only for upgrading and retraining but also for second chance general education. Unfortunately, any really serious provision of second chance general education in the third, fourth or fifth decades of life would be very costly, even if income maintenance costs could be reduced by redirecting social security payments at present supporting many millions of unemployed adults. The productivity yield would be very inadequate, unlike the highly focused training financed by employers. Equity suggests that provision for older adults, who received short measure when young, should be expanded. But the cost, in terms of a productive use of resources, measured by economic growth, would be high.

In a thoroughly gloomy analysis Becker explains the decline of educational investment in individuals as they grow older by (a) the decline in benefits from each subsequent expenditure as fewer years of life remain, and (b) the increase in investment costs for those in paid work because foregone earnings rise as human capital accumulates. On top of a reducing pay-back period and rising costs the very nature of human capital formation brings diminishing returns to increased spending. The embodiment of the capital in a person means that '... since the memory capacity, physical size, etc. of each investor is limited, eventually diminishing returns set in from producing additional capital. The result is increasing marginal costs of producing a dollar of returns'. (Becker, 1975, p. 98). Such 'explanations' of the decline of public educational spending with age are based on models made more manageable by assuming, for example, that there is no other motive for educational spending than to raise productivity or earnings, that earnings reflect marginal productivities and that public policy should be determined by marginal rates of return — if these could be measured. Nevertheless, moving from models to policy-making, most economists would argue for a concept of allocative or external efficiency which includes a well defined set of equity goals.

Positive and normative

The painter, David Hockney, likes to point out that things are never as they are, that the stylized is the real. In economics the facts, when there are any, are stylized. The notion that there are such things as value-free, 'objective' facts is an obvious fiction. In order to search out, select and interpret evidence, in order to make factual statements, the economist has to make assumptions about relationships, such as the connexions between teaching and learning, or between learning, labour productivity and earnings. It is increasingly difficult to establish reliably the nature of relationships between resources, process and outcomes. It cannot be said that we have a well-tested and effectively unchallenged 'positive' knowledge of them. So the economist has to deal with critical areas of ignorance by assuming that he knows what he does not know. He has to use knowledge assumptions, i.e. factual judgements that are in principle testable but in practice untestable.

In order to cope with this fundamental ignorance the economist has to make judgements of fact — informed guesses — which may be influenced by his own values. Ng has argued that 'value judgements proper and judgements of fact which reflect personal values are logically distinct; the one cannot, the other can be true or false'. (Ng, 1972, p.1015). He has proposed that these ignorance-coping judgements be called subjective judgements of fact and that the word 'value' be reserved for judgements which are in themselves statements of values. This produces a threefold classification

- factual judgements, descriptive of what is and therefore true or false

- subjective judgements of fact, logically similar but in practice untestable and vulnerable to the values of whoever makes the judgement

- value judgements, evaluative or prescriptive, which cannot be true or false in practice or in principle, only more or less persuasive.

The value assumptions which an economist uses are based on value judgements. These may be judgements about the value which households, enterprises, voluntary organisations or governments attach to the expenditure or receipt of one pound three, four or five years hence rather than now. They may be judgements about the value to be put on an educational use of the time of an employee, an unemployed or a retired person, or on the time of an employed person when he is not engaged in paid work.

The economist can offer some positive knowledge in the form of factual statements. His analysis can be objective in the sense that premises, logic and data are laid out in an open and challengeable way. In the analysis of educational issues it is difficult for him to avoid positive-type judgements which are liable to be influenced by his personal experiences as well as his preferences. He may even use value judgements to make straightforward statements about what ought to be. Unfortunately, most economic analysis of education does little to help readers to distinguish the crucially different status of these three types of judgement — factual, subjective, value — as they affect conclusions (positive statement). All economic analyses should do so (normative statement).

The distinction between the positive and the normative can be useful. For policy purposes, it is necessary to know both the present distribution of the cost burden (what is) and the distribution towards which public policy is working (what ought to be). The first task requires a positive investigation to unearth the facts; the second requires a definition of policy objectives which reflects a set of values.

Mere description of the role of government is a complex and difficult task. Government intervention occurs in three main modes

- regulation and control, sometimes to the extent of making purchase or provision compulsory (cf legislation on training for safety at work in many countries);

- taxation, followed by spending on educational services provided by public sector institutions;

- taxation, followed by subsidy of private sector educational services in order to lower prices to the learner to a level defined as socially optimal, i.e. where individual purchases of educational services reach a preordained level and distribution.

To move from a description of the way government actually operates in adult education to the way in which it ought to operate requires a crucial shift from a positive/descriptive model to a normative/prescriptive model. How far can the analyst go without pre-empting value-laden choices which properly belong to the adult learner or to the provider of other resources, whether that is a firm, an association, or government? The most that can be done, for example after describing how government presently operates, is to show what alternative actions are available and what are their likely consequences so that decision makers can see the likely implications of different preferences.

The development of industrial training policy in the United Kingdom since 1964 can be used to show how these distinctions between efficiency and equity and between the positive and the normative apply in practice. In Britain, provision of a major form of adult education like industrial training is the consequence of a complex set of decisions originating in firms, professional bodies, trade unions, voluntary associations, central government agencies and departments, local government and millions of households. The 1964 Industrial Training Act administered 'shock treatment' to industrial training, with considerable repercussions on many of the non-government decision makers. The Act sought

- to ensure an adequate supply of trained labour for the economy;
- to improve the quality and efficiency of trained labour;
- to share the cost of training more equitably between firms.

In practice, the efficiency objective of raising the rate of economic growth by increasing the quantity and quality of skilled workers proved to be paramount. The only equity objective related to the distribution of training costs between firms, and in many industries redistribution either did not occur or was negligible. The Act was aimed at firms and not directly at workers, so it developed an elaborate financial mechanism, with variations according to the industry, to earmark part of the cash flow of firms for approved training.

This 1964 Industrial Training Act was based on a positive diagnosis of an existing situation. In essence, an industrial training 'problem' was identified. The analysis was built on the positive hypothesis that skill shortages act as an important restraint on economic growth during periods of expansion, and that inadequate training contributes to these skill shortages. Moreover, this inadequate training was held to be due to the behaviour of some firms which, instead of training, poached trained workers from other and more virtuous firms. So the Act set up an institutional structure to monitor and if necessary adjust the distribution of training costs between firms in order to achieve an increased volume of better quality training, with the poachers financing training to a level comparable with that financed by the virtuous.

In 1973 the institutional mechanism was modified and added to by the Employment and Training Act. The official positive analysis was also revised, in the belief that the institutional structures designed to encourage firms to meet their own needs under the 1964 Act might still not secure a supply of skills adequate for national needs. So increasing amounts of centrally-earmarked tax funds were now injected into the training system.

By 1982 the official positive analysis had been revised yet again. In many industries, the levy-grant-exemption system for intervening in the financing of company training to ensure minimum levels and quality of training, introduced under the 1973 Act, seemed to have little potential for bringing about further change in quantity or quality. Indeed, many Industry Training Boards were handling more tax money on an agency basis, for interventions directed by the Manpower Services Commission, than levy money raised from firms in scope and redistributed throughout the industry.

Given this altered role of many Industry Training Boards by 1982, and diminished respect for the old equity objective of counteracting poaching, it was not surprising when all but seven ITBs were marked out for dissolution. In this way, the proportion of workers whose training is monitored or provided for through voluntary bodies and the market was enlarged from approximately 50 to 70 per cent of all employees. There was a reduction in the amount of government or industry-collective intervention in the decisions of firms as to the level and character of training to be financed out of their own cash flow. Under the 1964 Act, for many firms, control over their own training was, to a varying degree, constrained by the policy of an ITB or, from 1975, of the Manpower Services Commission. At the margin, for some firms, there was a redistribution of training costs. But after nearly twenty years a sizeable part of the ITB structure was dismantled or emasculated.

Reasons for these developments have been advanced. The span of history from the 1962 White Paper 'Training for the Future' to the 1981 Manpower Services Commission's 'Review of the Industrial Training Act' is replete with competing analyses of what is and what ought to be. The point to be made here is that each modification of financing arrangements was based on a positive analysis of the current situation and trends in industrial training, combined with a view as to who ought to pay for training. Critics of the official position offered an alternative positive analysis or took a different view as to who should pay.

CHAPTER TWO: A FOUR SECTOR INDUSTRY

NEW ACCOUNTING FRAMEWORKS

The sectoral structure

A standard method of classifying industries is to group production units according to the closeness of substitution between products which cater to essentially the same demand. The characteristic output of adult education is the skills, knowledge and values demanded by adult learners, using the word education to embrace activities which are often described as training. Provision for adult education, so conceived, can be thought of as an industry, in which resources in aid of learning are organised in four principal sectors. Each sector takes its character from a distinct decision unit or economic agency. These units are government, the enterprise, the parafisc, and the househould.

Funds flow to and between these decision units, and these flows may be studied at different stages

- according to their source;
- as they are allocated between educational and non-educational uses, and between different educational uses;
- as they are spent on educational purposes;
- according to use, when they finally bring together learners, teachers and all other resources in the actual processes of teaching and learning.

A two dimensional matrix (Figure 1, p.18) can be used to trace the flow of funds between the big four decision units, and through the four major financial functions of supply, allocation, expenditure and use of funds.

This analysis is concerned with financing people as well as financing organisations, even though the main classification is based on these decision-making organisations. The adult participates in two roles simultaneously, (1) as a learning member of one or more of the decision units — citizen, subscriber, employee, householder — and also (2) as a non-learner who nevertheless finds himself contributing

Figure 1: Flows of funds by sector

Function / Sector	Supply of funds	Allocation	Expenditure	Use
Government				
Parafiscal				
Corporate				
Household				

to the costs of, or sharing the benefits from, the learning of other adults.

The government sector is comprised of central and local government. The enterprise is the criterion unit for the corporate sector. It does not matter whether the enterprise is a single firm, or that collection of firms known as an industry, or a single firm industry; nor whether the enterprise is owned privately, co-operatively, or publicly. The parafisc is an institution typically financed from a number of quite different sources. On one side of the parafisc is government, raising funds very largely through taxation. On the other side are the for-profit education and training organisations which raise funds through sale of educational services, together with enterprises whose main business of selling non-educational goods and services generates the cash flow from which they finance their own educational and training activities. The parafiscal institution is an alternative means of arranging group financing of education. It is quite distinct from but not untouched by the tax-based or market-based arrangements which are central to government or corporate financing (see Clement, 1979). Frequently, the parafisc has several revenue sources, including some or all of

- government grants, loans and tax exemptions;

- statutory or voluntary levies, subscriptions and cash
  donations paid from corporate and household incomes;

- sales of services.

A parafisc is a non-government collective built around a smaller group
interest than the interest of an entire country. It may have education
or training as its exclusive function, for example the Fonds d'Assurance
Formation in France, or the Workers' Educational Association and the
Industry Training Boards in the United Kingdom. Its educational and
training activities may be a subsidiary function, as they are in many
professional associations, trades unions, political parties and churches.
It differs from the firm in that it is generally a non-profit organisation,
does not rely exclusively on a cash flow generated from the sale of non-
educational goods and services, and is not restricted to training
activities which serve the production needs of the enterprise.

The household is also distinct from the other decision units. It is either
one person living alone or a group of persons, who may or may not be
related, living at the same address and with common housekeeping.
Inheritance apart, its income is mostly generated from the sale of labour
services, and to a limited extent from the yield on investments or transfer payments from government, e.g. pensions and social security
benefits. Other decision units draw financial sustenance from the household in the form of taxes, subscriptions and the prices paid for the goods
and services it consumes. The household's disposable income constitutes a separate and independent capacity to finance adult learning which
is immense, underrated and under-researched.

In order to model the flow of funds within the education industry it is
convenient to conceptualise provision in terms of separate sectors. But
if the limited purpose of this model is forgotten it may obscure important
features of institutional behaviour. Whole public sector institutions or
parts of institutions may derive an important part of their income from
fees and gifts and generally behave like parafiscal organisations. Moreover, some institutions which are heavily tax-funded and are generally
regarded as public institutions, such as British universities, are legally
constituted as parafiscs. Division of suppliers into four sectors
simplifies a reality which is often a rather messy spectrum of institutional forms and a degree of role imitation between sectors.

The financing decisions of the four main decision units are generally
interdependent, so much so that it is difficult for policy-makers to

deploy a financial instrument in one sector, and to change the flow of funds, without repercussions in other sectors. At bottom, this inter-dependence springs from the availability of substitutes :

- outputs of the decision units, their educational services, can often be substituted for each other;

- one mix of sources of finance can sometimes be substituted for another combination;

- implicit expenditures may on occasion by substituted for explicit or cash spending, and vice versa.

This interdependence may be shown diagramatically by reference to Figures 2 and 3 on pages 21 and 22 (derived originally from Peacock, Glennerster and Lavers, 1968). These figures are little more than country applications of the empty matrix shown in Figure 1. The education to which Figures 2 and 3 refer is confined to structured learning which improves performance in a present or future job, both vocational preparation within the initial education system and continuing education and training within and beyond the formal education system (see their source, Drake and Rasmussen, 1981). To quantify even the major flows of funds mapped by Figures 2 and 3 would be a difficult task. Some years ago a systematic attempt was made to recalculate the often inconsistent public sector data for the United Kingdom and produce a consistent set of flow data for one year. One consequence of using consistent accounting procedures was that public spending on education amounted to one third less than the official esti-mate, 3.2 instead of 4.8 per cent of gross national product (Peacock, Glennerster and Lavers, 1968). But very substantial funds, with a degree of potential substitution, are undoubtedly transferred along these routes in Denmark and the United Kingdom. Recent estimates contain considerable margins of error. But in very broad magnitudes it seems that in the United Kingdom in 1977-78 some £4 billion to £4.5 billion was spent on training (Drake, 1980, Chapter 2). Of this total, perhaps £1.5 billion was spent on training during initial education, and most of that would be allocated from central and local tax revenues, to be spent and used by public authorities in publicly-maintained institutions — the top two lines in Figure 3. Around £2.8 billion was probably spent on post-initial training of adults in a wide variety of settings, most of the funds being allocated by enterprises, but some by parafiscs like the ITBs and also by households.

21

Figure 2. Operators of Training Finance in DK.

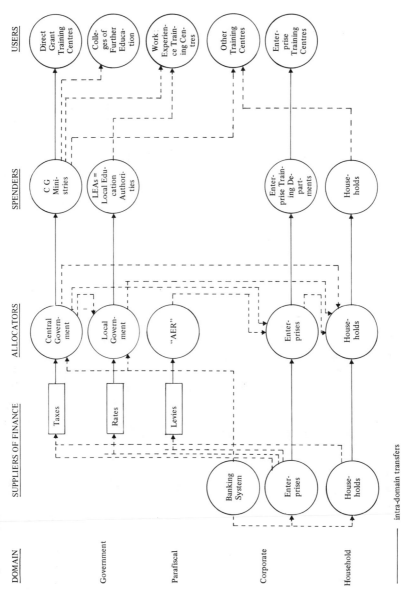

Figure 3. Operators of Training Finance in the UK.

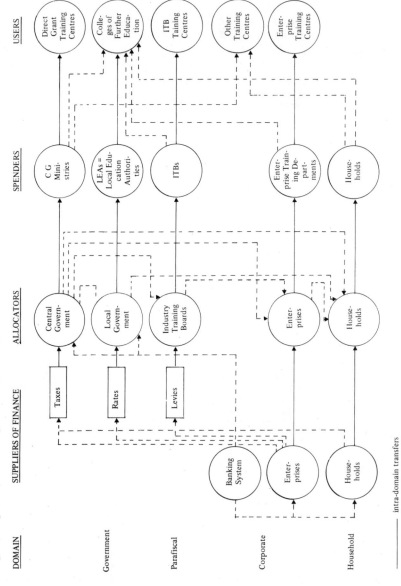

Political, economic and institutional differences between countries help to produce different ways of financing adult education, in respect of the flows of funds and the use of financial instruments. In the case of Denmark and the United Kingdom (see Drake and Rasmussen, 1981) it seems, on present knowledge, that Denmark may rely more heavily than Britain on governmental allocation, spending and use of funds, with correspondingly less reliance on the parafiscal sector, employers and for-profit suppliers of education and training for adults. Countries develop institutions specialised by function and for the circumstances within each country, for example, in industrial training, where the Arbejdsgivernes Elevrefusian (AER) and the Industry Training Board (ITB) are used in Figures 2 and 3 as illustrative parafiscal institutions. Countries also use different instruments to achieve the same purpose, Denmark leaning towards government-guaranteed bank loans in cases where the British tend to use central or local government grants to support trainees financially.

Any attempt to map and quantify the flows shown in Figures 2 and 3 raises questions about the incidence of financial costs of adult learning, and the reasons for different patterns of financing for different kinds of adult education. One of the reasons for the difficulty of answering such questions is the severity of data problems. In many instances, the original source of funds is by no means clear. For example, in Denmark and the United Kingdom the banking system can properly be regarded as an original supplier of funds for adult education. But it is a very different kind of supplier from enterprises or households. Bank lending to government in order to finance budget deficits is the basis of that creation of credit which permits enterprises and households, as well as government, to finance spending in excess of current income. However, such bank lending is rarely attributable to a specific expenditure like that on training: it simply enhances a general capacity to finance both educational and non-educational activities.

It is clear that central and local government and parafiscs are not original suppliers of funds: they depend on vertical, inter-domain transfers from enterprises, households and the banking system (see Figures 2 and 3). Many inter-domain transfers are not specific to adult education in the sense of being earmarked for that purpose. They are general transfers in the form of central or local taxes or loans. But there are education-specific transfers. Some of these are effectively hypothecated taxes. For example, in Denmark, the Arbejdsgivernes Elevrefusian, set up by Act of Parliament in 1977, has the power to raise revenue from almost all employers, who are already obliged to pay another parafisc a levy for supplementary old age pensions to wage and salary earners. Indeed, the training levy is fixed annually by the AER as a percentage of the supplementary pension levy, to which it is administratively connected. There is no comparable national parafisc in the United Kingdom. For three employees in every ten there are Industry Training Boards, which, within their own industry, have the power to levy a payroll tax on employers, and the power to exempt employers who are already spending on approved training of their own employees up to or beyond the yield of the training levy. Some transfers which are not taxes are effectively hypothecated, for example subscriptions and cash donations by households to exclusively educational parafiscs which are omitted from Figures 2 and 3 only for the sake of simplification.

If the financial function under consideration is not raising, but allocating, spending or using funds, then there are challenging differences between Denmark and the United Kingdom. For instance, intra-domain transfers at the governmental level are calculated using quite similar rules. In both countries central to local government transfers may be determined by a formula using need and resource criteria like length of road system, population, age structure and so forth. However, in Denmark the main spenders on further education colleges, as well as the allocators of tax funds, are central government ministries. For approved budgets, the users of funds — colleges of further education — receive direct from the Ministry of Education funds sufficient to charge zero fees to employers and to learners.

In the United Kingdom funding is more complex. The great bulk of educational funds from central government budgets is transferred in the form of a block grant to local authorities. Planned educational spending by local authorities is taken into account by central government in fixing the size of a total block grant, which is also used in aid of non-educational spending by local authorities. But no portion of the total block grant is specifically allocated to education, except for Northern Ireland, where the education and library boards are directly financed by the Department of Education for Northern Ireland. It is for local authorities to determine the allocation between educational and non-educational uses, and between competing educational uses, subject to the maintenance of those educational services which it is mandatory for them to finance. The legislation on local authority post-school provision, especially that which is not obviously job-related, is drawn in such a way that there is room

for considerable variation in expenditures on the education of adults.
These variations can be seen over time, but also at any one point of
time between the 113 fairly heterogeneous local authorities with educa-
tion responsibilities in the United Kingdom — the Inner London
Education Authority, 20 Outer London Boroughs, 30 English Shire
Counties, 36 Metropolitan Districts in England, 8 Welsh Counties, the
Isles of Scilly, 9 Scottish Regional Authorities, 3 Scottish Island
Authorities and 5 Education and Library Boards in Northern Ireland.
The further education colleges in Great Britain draw a growing propor-
tion of their revenue from fees (1) paid out of tax funds by the Manpower
Services Commission, (2) paid indirectly or directly by employers,
and (3) paid by adult learners out of the disposable income of their
households.

The sheer difference in scale between the Danish and British economies,
and the relatively small size of industrial enterprises in Denmark,
seems to be one of the main reasons for the differences between the two
countries in the proportion of funds for off-the-job training which comes
from taxes and from the cash flow of firms, and also for the different
uses to which funds are put by the colleges. More than has usually been
the case in England and Wales, Danish colleges try to specialise
between themselves in the training needs of clusters of trades or industries. In some cases they then perform a highly specialised role not
dissimilar to that of a training centre run by an ITB, such as the
Construction Industry Training Centre at Bircham Newton in England.

Financing behaviour of sectors

Policy-making requires an operational definition of goals, a clear view
of what ought to be, i.e. what is the preferred educational provision,
the preferred level and pattern of funding, the preferred incidence of
cost and benefit. But, in order to be effective, any reforms need to be
grounded in a knowledge of what is, a knowledge of the present flow of
funds and of the operation of financial instruments which influence the
direction and magnitude of these flows.

Very little systematic work has yet been done in order to understand the
interdependent behaviour of the decision units. Some of the most
productive investigations are those by Burton Weisbrod and his associates
in the United States (Weisbrod, 1977). These investigators have produced a theoretically-based definition and measurement of the whole
education industry. Weisbrod began to investigate the hypothesis that

the government and the voluntary sectors of this industry will produce
similar collective-consumption goods, while the private, for-profit
sector will produce private-good substitutes for the collective goods
produced by the other two sectors.

Pure collective goods, also known as pure public goods, are goods
where the benefit cannot be assigned and charged to an individual
consumer. As usual, the word 'good' comprehends both services and
material products, just as the word 'education' comprehends training.
The demand for pure collective goods may not be at all the same from
individual to individual, but consumption is unavoidable, joint and equal
between individuals. The more there is for one person — defence, for
example — the more there is for another, whether this other wants it or
even contributes to its cost. With a private good, the more there is for
one the less there is for another. Collectiveness is a quality of the good,
a property of its supply. It does not tell us anything about the ownership
of the means of producing the good. Collective goods need not be produced by publicly-owned enterprises, though the nature of pure collective
goods is such that it is impossible or difficult to finance their production
without relying on taxation.

The degree of collectiveness of any good lies along a continuum between
a pure collective good and a pure private good. It is essential to think
in terms of degree of collectiveness and not in terms of a sharp
dichotomy between two different kinds of good, collective and private.
The degree of collectiveness of educational services is critical, because
it affects the feasibility of using different methods to finance provision.
Goods of any degree of collectiveness can be financed out of taxation,
subject only to the electorate's willingness to bear the tax burden. But
pure collective goods cannot be financed out of prices and subscriptions,
and quasi-collective goods can be difficult to finance simply out of subscriptions and donations. So price financing and tax financing are not
perfectly substitutable for each other. The character of the educational
service, and especially the incidence of the benefits, may constrain the
choice of financial instruments.

If the collectiveness continuum is envisaged as divided into three bands,
pure collective, quasi-collective/quasi-private, and pure private goods,
then a great many educational services will be found somewhere within
the intermediate band of quasi-collective/quasi-private goods. That is
to say, there are frequently very clear benefits which can be allocated
to individual consumers. These are for their exclusive consumption:

other would-be consumers can be excluded. Because of these strong
private good characteristics the production of educational services for
adults can be, and often is, financed by means of market-type financial
instruments like user charges or subscriptions. The costs can be
charged to individual beneficiaries because many or all of the benefits
can be sold exclusively to them. However, even where educational
services do have strong private good characteristics, they may also
have other collective good characteristics. The extent and nature of
these collective good characteristics is sometimes a matter of controversy, not least because it influences the way in which their production is financed. To the extent that these services produce benefitis
which spillover to people other than the adult learner, and for which it
is not feasible to charge, a degree of tax financing may be justified.
Certainly, it would be impossible to argue that all public spending on
education and training of adults is spending on pure collective goods,
i.e. where benefits cannot be allocated to individuals, charging is
impracticable and the case for tax-financing is overwhelming (see
Seldon, 1977, Chapter 3). It is equally certain that adult educational
services are often not a pure private good. So the scope for mixed
modes of financing is extensive.

A finer discrimination between types of adult education than the simple
three-fold classification — collective, quasi-collective, private — is
possible and necessary in order to understand choice of financing modes.
Some quasi-collective educational services provide benefits which spill
over indiscriminately to those in the geographical neighbourhood of the
adult learner or to the entire national community. Forms of adult
education which increase social cohesion, socialise adult immigrants
into the host community or enrich a community's cultural base might be
included in this class. Other quasi-collective educational services are
more selectively collective. That is to say, they are collective only for
a discrete group within the population, such as members of a craft, a
profession, a church or a trade union. Parafiscs cater particularly for
such interest groups, sometimes in parallel or in co-operation with
government-provided and tax-financed education, sometimes in a unique
operation. Some of the benefits from the educational services of these
parafiscs are of direct, private advantage to subscribing members;
other benefits accrue to the whole membership as spillovers or neighbourhood effects.

Weisbrod has proposed a rough financial measure of the degree of
collectiveness of an organisation's output. According to this, an

organisation providing purely private goods — where all the benefits are captured by definable individual consumers — will have revenue only from sales of services and from member subscriptions or dues. An organisation which provides only pure collective goods — collective goods in the strict sense — will be heavily or entirely dependent on gifts or on grants from tax funds. One rough measure of the degree of collectiveness in the output of an organisation would then be the proportion of its total revenue coming from gifts and grants (Weisbrod, 1977, p.173).

Weisbrod (1977, p.102) goes on to hypothesise that the government sector will provide collective goods of the quantity and quality demanded by the median voter, while the voluntary sector will contribute to the meeting of demand for collective goods that exceeds the demand of the median voter. Whether or not this is so, and can be shown to be so, is yet to be demonstrated. But the attempt to formulate hypotheses which relate to the sources of funds and the financing behaviour of organisations is vital if systematic and positive knowledge of education and training finance is to be built up.

Such attempts are not new among economists. Gary Becker (1975, p.26) developed an important distinction between general and specific training:

> 'Completely general training increases the marginal productivity of trainees by exactly the same amount in the firms providing training as in other firms. Clearly some kinds of training increase productivity by different amounts in the firms providing training and in other firms. Training that increases productivity more in firms providing it will be called specific training. Completely specific training can be defined as training that has no effect on the productivity of trainees that would be useful in other firms. Much on-the-job training is neither completely specific nor completely general but increases productivity more in the firms providing it and falls within the definition of specific training. The rest increases productivity by at least as much in other firms and falls within a definition of general training.'

He went on to advance propositions about the conditions under which and the ways in which costs would be shared between firms and workers, depending on the nature of training, i.e. whether it was specific or general. Where the training was completely specific all the benefits could be captured by the firm and it would be in the interest of the firm to finance it. To the extent that the benefits were general and so could be enjoyed by the individual after leaving the training firm, then it might be in the interest of the individual to finance the training by accepting very low wages during training, but it would not be in the interest of the firm to finance it. A hypothesis of this kind can be treated as a positive one and evidence can be collected to see whether or not it accurately describes the financing behaviour of firms or of workers (see Oatey, 1970; Ryan, 1980). It can even be converted into a normative hypothesis, which says that costs should be shared between participants in this way or that.

At this point, the feature to note about Weisbrod's hypothesis concerning government and voluntary sector activities, and Becker's hypothesis concerning corporate and worker financing of training, is that they exemplify productive bases for positive investigations of financing behaviour. What is learned, who is affected by this learning, and the nature of these effects are regarded as critical determinants in decisions about financing.

Flows of funds analysis: an American illustration

In carrying out a flows of funds analysis for the entire education industry of the United States for the fiscal year 1970 Bendick (Weisbrod, 1977, Chapter 5) distinguished four types of instruction, that in early childhood, that of children, that for youth, and finally postsecondary and adult education. He used a broad accounting convention which traces the flow of implicit as well as of cash revenues. Cash revenues are simply the transfer payments and payments in exchange for resources and goods which are normally thought of as the entire data of financial analysis, and which flow between government, parafiscs, firms and households. Implicit revenues are hypothetical flows, where no actual cash transaction or book-keeping entries have occurred. A valuation is made of these hypothetical flows, and entered into the accounts alongside actual flows. The reasoning is that hypothetical and actual flows interact, and that hypothetical flows affect decisions about the amount and type of education in a similar way to actual flows. It is not uncommon in military training accounts for the wage costs of trainees to be included in training costs. No-one argues that civilian employers are unaware of these wage costs just because it is quite common, in some countries or industries, not to include them in civilian training accounts. Imputation simply recognises that awareness and makes for comparability between training in military and civilian employment.

It is not so much variations of costing practice which cause problems. It is the eccentricity and inconsistency of some of these variations. Sometimes hypothetical flows are valued because it is recognised that it is almost accidental that a scarce resource used in adult education has not been bought and sold so that no market measure has been generated. An employer may calculate all the cash costs of an in-house training programme for employees and then estimate output lost by multiplying the hourly labour cost of the employees against the number of training hours, on the assumption that the employees are paid roughly what they are worth in terms of output. Often, the value of trainee time is ignored in any accounting, even though, as an implicit cost, it would constitute a big fraction of the sum of explicit and implicit training costs. When adult education outside the hours of paid work is being costed, it is common to ignore the time of the adult learner and effectively value it at zero. Yet this learner time is a scarce resource which has valuable alternative uses. Whenever cost-influenced choices are investigated time should be costed, and especially in the case of adult learners, where there is often scope for the adult to substitute between money and time costs when trying to acquire skills and knowledge.

The implicit cost of learner time is frequently the major element in the cost of adult learning. But it is by no means the only example of an implicit cost. Adult education which takes place in buildings or with equipment which is fully amortised is rarely costed to include a valuation of that physical capital, for example at replacement cost (see Drake, 1971 and 1972). The voluntary services of teachers and instructors, given to educational organisations such as churches and professional associations, are rarely costed, even though the implicit cost of those services can be one of the largest elements in the total economic cost. Between 1975-76 and 1977-78 an adult literacy campaign was aimed at Britain's two million adult illiterates by the BBC and an Adult Literacy Resource Agency. Between them they put more than £4 million into the project, with significant further spending by local authority, education and library services. But one of the major and unaccounted costs was the implicit cost of the time of 80,000 volunteer tutors in England and Wales. Over the three years, these tutors gave freely of their services, sometimes on a 1 :1 basis in the home, in order to help some 125,000 men and women. Voluntary services may be substituted for those bought in the market, so a partial accounting which recognises only cash expenditures will under-record the teaching resources committed to adult education by the value of these voluntary services.

All those examples relate to scarce resources which are committed to adult learning but often go unrecorded. The flows of resources into educational uses are real enough. Strictly, it is the shadow valuations put upon them in order to calculate implicit revenue or implicit cost

which are hypothetical. However, there is another and different kind
of implicit revenue. This is a tax expenditure. In Britain it often takes
the form of exemption of educational institutions with charitable status
from corporation, capital gains or capital transfer taxation, and exemption of the same institutions from part of the local property tax known
as 'the rates'. The value of these exemptions measures a commitment
of resources to education in the sense that part of the cash flow of these
institutions is not diverted into tax payments. It becomes available,
and is effectively earmarked by public policy, only because it will be
devoted to educational uses and purposes beneficial to the community.
When tax for which educational institutions would otherwise be liable is
not charged this is equivalent, in its effect on the allocation of resources
between educational and non-educational uses, to public spending on
education. For this reason, in a broad accounting such as that used by
Bendick, it is added to other implicit expenditures to form what he calls
implicit revenues.

The effects of a more comprehensive accounting framework are
dramatic. They reveal explicit expenditures in a perspective which is
not only quite different from conventional government accounting but
more relevant for understanding and taking many financing decisions.
In making his cautious estimates of the size and structure of the entire
American education industry, Bendick illustrates the differences
between a conventional and a more comprehensive accounting framework.

Three major features of Bendick's accounting frame (see Tables 1 and 2)
may influence an analysis of the financing of adult education in any
country. One is the scope of his preferred definition of education; the
second is the analysis by sectors; and the third is the inclusion of
implicit alongside explicit revenues.

If the United States Office of Education definition of education is used,
postsecondary and adult education comprises education in colleges and
universities and avocational adult schools and lessons. However,
Bendick applies the rule that educational activities which can be substituted for each other, because they perform similar functions, should be
included together. For this reason he adds in proprietary postsecondary
vocational schools, military education and instruction by employers.
His accounting is still conservative. For example, he probably does
not include all education in parafiscal organisations or all on-the-job
training. But the proprietary schools do include for-profit trade,
technical and business schools; the military education includes both

Table 1 Enrollment and Revenues for all Systematic Instruction by Type of Instruction, United States, Fiscal Year 1970

Type of Instruction	Full time equivalent enrollment (a)		Cash Revenues (b)		Implicit Revenues (c)		All Revenues (d)	
	Enrollment '000s	% of total	Revenues $m	% of total	Net revenue $m	% of total	Revenues $m	% of total
1. Early childhood instruction	1,632	3.6	2,108	3.2	115	0.1	2,223	1.5
2. Instruction for children (e)	23,838	52.1	25,859	39.3	2,811	3.4	28,670	19.2
3. Instruction for youth (f)	10,990	24.0	17,114	26.0	32,781	39.3	49,895	33.4
4. Postsecondary and adult instruction	9,318	20.4	20,744	31.5	47,680	57.2	68,424	45.9
(i) College & university	4,964	10.8	13,694	20.8	23,994	28.8	37,688	25.3
(ii) Proprietary vocational schools	1,122	2.5	1,485	2.3	5,068	6.1	6,553	4.4
(iii) Instruction in the military	574	1.3	3,678	5.6	868	1.0	4,546	3.0
(iv) Instruction by employers	1,597	3.5	821	1.2	10,553	12.7	11,374	7.6
(v) Avocational adult schools and lessons	1,061	2.3	1,066	1.6	7,197	8.6	8,263	5.5
Total: all conventional instruction	38,824	84.8	56,562	85.9	55,663	66.8	112,225	75.2
Total: all systematic instruction	45,778	100.0	65,825	100.0	83,387	100.0	149,212	100.0

(a) Full time equivalency is 2028 person-hours per year.
(b) Government expenditures, tuition and fees, and gross cash donations.
(c) Labour donations (voluntary services), tax exemptions and student time.
(d) Cash revenue plus value of labour donations, tax exemptions and student time.
(e) Grades 1-8 or ages 6-14
(f) Grades 9-12 or ages 15-18

Source: Derived from Table 5-7, Marc Bendick, Jr., 'Education as a Three Sector Industry' in Burton A. Weisbrod, The Voluntary Non-Profit Sector, Lexington Books, 1977.

Table 2: Total revenues, funded and unfunded, for systematic instruction in postsecondary and adult instruction, by producing sector, United States Fiscal Year 1970

Type of Instruction	Government sector Revenue $m	(a) % of sector	% of type	Voluntary sector Revenue $m	(a) % of sector	% of type	For-Profit sector Revenue $m	(a) % of sector	% of type
(i) Colleges and universities	26,875	27.0	71.3	10,813	46.1	28.7	0	0	0
(ii) Proprietary vocational schools	0	0	0	0	0	0	6,553	25.1	100.0
(iii) Instruction in the military	4,546	4.6	100.0	0	0	0	0	0	0
(iv) Instruction by employers	559	0.6	4.9	0	0	0	10,815	41.4	95.1
(v) Avocational adult schools and lessons	139	0.1	1.7	2,579	11.0	31.1	5,545	21.2	67.2
Total postsecondary and adult instruction	32,119	32.2	46.9	13,392	57.1	19.6	22,913	87.7	33.5

(a) Percentage of sector contribution to all systematic instruction, i.e. all education as conventionally defined by the US Office of Education plus religious part-time schools for children and youth, educational activities of out-of-school groups, part-time speciality schools, proprietary vocational schools, education in the military, and classes by civilian employers.

Source: Table 5-8, Marc Bendick, Jr., op. cit.

basic and specialist training; and employer instruction includes not
only apprenticeship but other kinds of formalised employee instruction.

Recognition of these three additional types of adult education is quantitatively important. Table 1 shows that the three types together account
for 35 per cent of full time equivalent enrollment at this level and 7 per
cent of such enrollments throughout a comprehensively defined education
system. Funding these three types of instruction requires 29 per cent
of cash revenues at this level and 33 per cent of the sum of explicit and
implicit revenues. Policy making has to recognise the reality of
substitutions between adult learning in different instructional modes
and organisational contexts. The appropriate definitions of adult education are the ones which recognise the substitutions by going beyond
conventionally-defined, bureaucratically-determined definitions to give
a policy-relevant picture of existing educational resource allocations
and of the actual educational options for adults.

Bendick is also able to show the importance for adult learners of non-
government provision (Table 2). Even his expanded definition of adult
education excludes structured or unstructured learning-by-doing at work,
and unsupervised self-instruction outside the environment of paid work.
So it falls very far short of covering the entire range of learning opportunities for adults and the resources available to assist such learning.
Nevertheless, using his semi-comprehensive definition, he is able to
show at least something of the financial significance of provision by
voluntary non-profit organisations and for-profit institutions. His non-
profit sector accounts for 20 per cent of explicit plus implicit revenues
at this level, the for-profit sector for another 34 per cent and the
remaining 47 per cent is attributable to the government sector. Not
surprisingly, government funding is dominant in the two types of adult
instruction which lie within the bureaucratic, U.S. Office of Education
definition of postsecondary and adult education. But this is due largely
to the government (or taxpayer) providing 71 per cent of all explicit and
implicit revenues for universities and colleges. In the armed forces,
100 per cent of funding comes from taxation. But the voluntary, non-
profit sector accounts for 29 per cent of all revenues for colleges and
universities and 31 per cent for avocational adult schools and lessons.
The for-profit sector not only finances proprietary schools 100 per cent
and employers' instruction 95 per cent; it also provides 67 per cent of
all revenues committed to avocational adult schools and lessons against
a mere 2 per cent from government.

The inclusion of implicit revenues within the accounting frame easily triples spending at this level, when that is measured only by government spending, fees and gross cash donations (see Table 1). Far and away the most important implicit revenue is that which values commitment of time by adult learners. This frequently accounts for over half of the sum of implicit and explicit revenues, while the other implicit revenues measured by Bendick — tax expenditures and labour donations — are of minor importance by comparison with the value of learner time or explicit revenues. One effect of this more thorough accounting is to show that in fiscal year 1970 the postsecondary and adult level of the United States education system was absorbing 46 per per cent of the entire system's explicit and implicit revenues, although conventional accounting showed it to be absorbing only 32 per cent of the system's cash revenues. Another effect of this more comprehensive accounting is to reveal part of the true significance of households and of their individual members in the financing of adult education, through the payment of fees, through donations in cash or in kind (voluntary services), and above all through the commitment of scarce learner time which has alternative and valuable uses. It also gives an indication of the extent to which the conventional accounting of government bureaucracies systematically overrates the importance of the government sector in the education of adults and underrates the non-profit voluntary and for-profit sectors.

Limitations and challenges

Unless they are empowered to innovate as a result of political decisions and the exercise of political will, government bureaucracies in developed countries have to do their best with the data and accounting systems which are available. In recent years there have been several path-breaking attempts, outside these bureaucracies, to develop accounting frameworks which are more helpful to policymakers than existing frameworks, and to fill these new frameworks with data (e.g. Machlup, 1962; Peacock, Glennerster and Lavers, 1968; Bendick, 1977). These new frameworks have their defects, but that is no reason to allow the perfect to be the enemy of the good. The existence of such frameworks constitutes a powerful challenge to the almost unchanged accounting systems of the government bureaucracies in most developed countries. These new frameworks provide rich exemplars for further investigations, especially in adult education, where the differences in coverage and in magnitudes of expenditure between conventional and new accounting frames are greater than for any other level of an education system. In other words, the conventional accounting has always been more deficient and irrelevant in adult education than elsewhere, and the scope for improvement in the quality and quantity of information is correspondingly large.

The mappings shown in Figures 2 and 3 are great simplifications. They are essentially illustrative. Even the quantitative tour de force performed by Marc Bendick involved the neglect of aspects of adult education whose importance he readily acknowledges. More comprehensive accounting quickly runs into all kinds of complexities. Some types of financial transfer involve international and inter-institutional book-keeping complexities so great that two dimensional figures seem quite inadequate for the task. For example, the Social Fund of the European Community provides member states with a level of governmental allocation of funds which is quite distinct from each country's own central and local government structures. Social Fund rules mean that a member state's central government can attract Social Fund monies to a training programme which central government establishes or approves. For example, at the enterprise level, £7.5 million can be allocated by the Social Fund to the government-approved British Shipbuilders' training scheme. The operation of the Social Fund means that some national tax funds are in effect earmarked for training purposes by the European Community. This is one of the most certain methods by which a national government can ensure the repatriation of some of the national payment to the Community budget, even though the procedure requires a matching contribution from national tax funds which has not been on a detour through Brussels.

Some of the practical difficulties of a more comprehensive accounting stem from book-keeping problems with financial transfers like those of the Social Fund or financial transfers between sectors. Other difficulties arise from severe shortages of data about the financing and resourcing of the less formal varieties of adult education such as structured on-the-job learning or private learning projects outside the hours of paid work. To develop and bring into operation improved accounting systems is so expensive of money and time there have to be solid and considerable benefits in prospect. In adult education there would be a dramatic improvement in coverage of policy-relevant data on finance and resources. The degree of substitutability between educational services for adults provided by different organisations, or in different instructional modes, offers a powerful tool for developing a more comprehensive and relevant accounting definition of adult education, and one which includes all four economic agencies in adult education, government, the parafisc, the firm and the household. These redefinitions, together with the elimination of the greatest source of measurement error by including instead of excluding implicit spending, have profound consequences for our understanding of the size and shape of the adult education industry and of policy options in adult education.

Not all these consequences will be welcome. Bendick (1977, p.140) has argued that these broader definitions and measurements may reduce many estimates of the social return on investment in education by as much as one third, and alter the relative rates of return to education at different ages or levels, and in different instructional modes. Of course, this argument assumes that while the costs of adult education are, in effect, revalued upwards — their true magnitude is recognised — the definition and measurement of its benefits, mostly in terms of education-related earnings differentials, can safely be left unchanged.

CHAPTER THREE: THE PUBLIC SECTOR: CENTRAL AND
LOCAL GOVERNMENT

GOVERNMENT INTERVENTIONS : PURPOSES

The rationale for government interventions in adult education, and the
methods of intervention, have been and remain matters of controversy.
The reasons for intervention fall into two distinct categories, those
concerned with one feature of adult education, its spillover effects on
people other than the learner, and all other reasons.

Spillover effects from adult education

Effects which are experienced by people other than the adult learner
are variously described by economists as spillover, neighbourhood or
external effects. If they are negative — disliked by the person or
organisation experiencing the effect — they are known as external costs.
If they are positive and welcome, they are known as external benefits.

The pure collective goods referred to in Chapter Two are merely
extreme or limiting cases of goods with external effects. Pure collective goods are consumption goods with effects from which people cannot
be excluded, and which people consume jointly and not at each other's
expense. Many educational services are partial collective goods. That
is to say, they have some external effects, and sometimes these may
even predominate over any private good characteristics, i. e. effects
from which people can be excluded and for which they can be charged.
It may be the use of resources by an individual learner (consumption),
or the activities of a supplier of educational services (production),
which generates costs for others which cannot be charged to that
learner or to that supplier: external costs. It may be that the adult's
learning yields benefits to other individuals or to organisations for
which it is not feasible to charge: external benefits. By definition,
these externalities are costs which do not influence the behaviour of the
person or organisation which generates them or benefits which, being
unmarketable, are not reflected in the market price of an educational
service.

If these externalities, negative or positive, are a significant feature of an educational service, no amount of institutional ingenuity can contrive a market which will produce an optimum supply of the service, i.e. where resource allocation is determined by all costs and benefits. The market will fail to articulate and strike a compromise between the preferences of all who share the cost and benefit consequences of some-one's learning; and the market is a financing mechanism which steers the allocation of a much larger set of resources than those which are purchased in the market. If the educational service has strong negative externalities — heavy external costs — market financing will tend to over-supply the service because suppliers do not bear all the costs nor reflect them fully in their (rather low) prices. If there are strong posi-tive externalities — a high level of external benefits — a market will tend to under-supply the service because some of those who clearly benefit from the service do not express demand for this provision by purchasing the service, signalling their preference and satisfaction, and providing suppliers with extra resources with which to increase provision.

It is one thing to define externality and its extreme case, the pure collective good. But it is quite another matter to identify and rank actual educational services according to the magnitude and sign (positive or negative) of the externalities associated with them. It is very difficult, with most educational services, (1) to measure the size and incidence of external effects, and (2) to value these effects. To a large extent, such benefits exist in the eye of the beholder (see Breneman and Nelson, 1981, Chapter 2). These difficulties of measurement and valuation lead to long-running controversies and to a situation where, as Peston (1972, p.19) points out, it is one objective of political activity to agree which goods are to be treated as collective or quasi-collective goods.

In other words, positive investigation is quite unable to produce defini-tive, objective measures of negative or positive external effects from an educational activity. It is widely accepted that there are such effects. Mandatory consumption requirements — safety training and industrial relations training for trade union officials — and the use of tax funds in many types of adult provision show how governments decide, normatively, which external effects should be ignored, which should be the subject of some kind of community control or action, and what form that inter-vention should take. Charity law applies to the educational activities of a wide range of organisations. It exemplifies long-run intervention to encourage activities because of the community's desire to enjoy the

external benefits which are believed to flow from education. Subsidies
to the visual and performing arts are another example.

Services which generate external benefits may be provided privately,
for instance by parafiscs, with or without financial encouragement by
government. Even if government remains netural, as long as adults
are prepared to pay the asking price or the subscription for the private
benefits which they can capture for themselves, they may support
provision which allows non-payers a 'free ride', i.e. to enjoy external
benefits without contributing to the cost of generating them. On the
other hand, one man's meat may be another man's poison. Some people
will not want or will abhor the spillover effects which others regard as
beneficial. If they cannot avoid these effects, they are 'forced riders'
rather than 'free riders'.

In education it is rarely the case that there will be no provision at all
unless government intervenes with tax financing. At most, education
may have some collective good characteristics and therefore can be
undersupplied unless tax funds are used to supplement market financing.
However, it is sometimes an open question whether the external benefits
are more significant than the external costs of education. That judgement depends on the ideological position of the person who is evaluating
the externalities as well as on the actual effects. A deschooler tends to
emphasise negative externalities associated with education. Spillovers
from education are regarded as a constraint on people's capacity to
develop their real potential (see Illich, 1970; Goodman, 1971; Reimer,
1971). Analysts with Marxist sympathies stress the role of educational
institutions in reproducing the distributions of political power, income
and wealth which foster and reinforce social inequality (see Bowles and
Gintis, 1976; Carnoy and Levin, 1976; Apple, 1982). The students of
credentialism document the progress of the diploma disease, a massive
external cost, which traps learners in a fiercely competitive game of
beggar-my-neighbour. This drives up and up the qualification — price
attached to occupational and social status. It misallocates resources
into more and more expensive screening procedures, to which the
content of education becomes subordinate (Berg, 1971; Wiles, 1974;
Dore, 1976; Hirsch, 1977).

The social pathology of contemporary educational systems, expounded
by deschoolers, Marxists and credentialists, shows how many people
consider the negative externalities or external costs of education to be
very significant. The interventions they have in mind do not spring from

a judgement that education is under-supplied because resource allocation is unresponsive to its huge external benefits. They are more likely to conclude that, on balance, the education on offer is over-supplied.

These analysts are looking to wholesale reforms of the entire structure of formal education, though each group wants a different set of reforms. Their debates frequently take place in compartments sealed off from each other and from the compartment in which other economists discuss the nature, magnitude and valuation of external benefits, while ignoring external costs. Adults who gain from beneficial spillovers will, on the whole, tend to avoid contributing towards their cost unless they are coerced, by taxation. Some economists favour massive tax support for most kinds of education. Often this is because they believe that education generates external benefits so large that they may even exceed in value the benefits which are separable and private to those who are being educated (e.g. Vaizey, 1972). Others are generally more sceptical about their size and value, especially the more diffuse and difficult-to-quantify external benefits such as crime reduction, enhanced political stability, social cohesion and cultural enrichment (see Blaug, 1970, pp 99-114).

The measurement of external effects is controversial because it is technically extremely difficult and it is vulnerable to ideological bias. But no one takes exception to the view that such effects constitute a ground for public intervention because of unavoidable limitations in the market mechanism. A wide variety of external benefits are alleged to flow from adult education programmes, for example increased learning by children from educating their parents, more efficient operation of labour markets, the socialisation of immigrant families from educating immigrant mothers, higher earnings for other members of a production team in which one person undergoes further training.

In OECD countries the state has a strong interest in producing informed voters, responsible neighbours and well behaved citizens. It is common for economists (e.g. Edding, 1981, p.124) to argue that recurrent education for vocational purposes requires only marginal or occasional public intervention because it mostly benefits employer and employee; similarly with recurrent education for self-enrichment, which serves personal interests. But Edding puts political education in an entirely different category, with the state playing an important part in its organisation and finance. In OECD countries it is in the interests of all to have well-informed and far-sighted electorates. But many individuals may not yet see it as being in their private interest to support from their after-tax income appropriate educational initiatives. This is the case for tax support of public service broadcasting, full and accurate reporting of political news, voluntary associations devoted to political education, and the incorporation of political education components into a wide range of adult education and training courses.

Production or consumption of almost any educational service is likely to have some spillover effects into the lives of people other than the learner. If governments were to intervene by providing, or regulating consumption of educational services whenever an external effect was identified, and a market failure diagnosed, there would be total and unending government intervention in all aspects of adult education. Stronger justification is required than the presence of external effects, if only because government allocation is as prone to failure as market allocation. The alternative to the market is the political process, which is not necessarily a superior means of dealing with the non-revelation of preferences by those experiencing the very effects which cause markets to fail. Governments are not necessarily better informed about the nature and incidence of external effects than private decisionmakers; and the incentive structures in government bureau-cracies may be no more appropriate than those in markets (see Sowell, 1980, Chapter 1). In most OECD countries naive interventionism has discredited itself, and the trend of opinion is towards greater caution. Government intervention remains the only remedy for market failure, so the only solution to the problem of allocative failures is to improve the design and execution of public interventions.

Other reasons for government intervention

Government intervention is not confined to supplying pure or partial collective goods. Governments subsidise non-government suppliers of collective goods. They transfer purchasing power between individuals, disbursing tax funds in the form of grants, scholarships, subsidised loans and pensions. Out of tax funds they also provide some private goods. Indeed, it has been estimated that in the United Kingdom in 1974 some £16,698 million, 40 per cent of total government spending and 22 per cent of gross national product, was devoted to goods and services, including education, with substantially or wholly separable benefits. These are mostly private goods for which charging is often practicable (Seldon, 1977, Table B).

Public policy has to decide upon a level and distribution of consumption of adult education services which is considered optimal for the whole society, i.e. which maximises the community's welfare, however government defines this. The identification of this level and distribution is not made explicit; but it is implicit in government interventions to change existing levels and distributions. How much of education-the-private-good should be produced in the whole community? Should its production be left to the private sector? Should its production in the private sector be subsidised? Should there be public sector production? Granted that some adult education services generate some external benefits, how much and what kind of beneficial spillovers should be financed out of tax funds?

These questions are answered very differently by sceptics and by enthusiasts. For instance, the sceptics do not share the enthusiastic belief in the availability of massive and widespread external benefits from increased provision of adult education. They tend to point out that private spending on education not only increases with disposable income; it tends to rise faster than the rate of increase in disposable income. So, education spending is likely to increase unaided as a proportion of total consumer spending if there is any economic growth and any increase in personal disposable incomes. This seems to be generally true of education spending by OECD governments over time; and it may also be true for spending by firms and households. Not only will private spending rise as incomes rise; disposable time expands as working hours are reduced and unemployment increases. Therefore, money and time devoted to adult learning could increase without increased public spending.

More specifically, Blaug (1981, p.575) has argued that in present conditions of supply, most of the demand for adult education, apart from firm-specific or occupation-specific training, is a demand for 'recreational' education from the ever-growing middle classes. Given the nature of what is on offer, 'there is absolutely no evidence of any learning demand on the part of adult workers for formal education of either the short-cycle or long-cycle variety'. Blaug's initial qualification is crucial. He advances the proposition that 'the character of adult education is more determined by the nature of its supply than by the nature of its demand' (Blaug, 1981, p.575). The extensive firm-specific training of adults in England and Wales (see Killeen and Bird, 1981) is a case in point. What Blaug doubts is the existence of an independent demand for paid educational leave in the form of leave for full-time general education without employer direction. Others have argued that the demand for this kind of general education is quite circumscribed. The financing of general adult education, in England and Wales, has been based squarely on the funding of organisations like local education authorities, universities and the Workers' Educational Association rather than financing the adult learner. The consequent lack of consumer power helped to produce a supplier-dominated service. With a few notable exceptions, it tends to be really congenial only to those who have become habituated to the teaching methods used, with rather limited success, on children, adolescents and very young adults, i.e. in the initial education system.

Enthusiasts often counter these sceptical observations with the argument that demand and supply are not independent of each other, in the way economists often assume, and that demand is constrained by supply. If only a small fraction of the population continues in full time education after the end of compulsory schooling, as is the case in England and Wales, it is only to be expected that subsequent demand for education will tend to be limited to this fraction of relatively well educated adults.

Some enthusiasts argue that it is lack of resourced and suitably pack-aged learning opportunities which inhibits demand. Others put forward a fundamentally different argument. They do not believe that it is mainly supply-side restrictions which hold back the expansion of educational provision for adults, that adults want to learn more but are inhibited by lack of resources. They believe that, although this constraint exists, the main inhibition comes from a genuine lack of demand by many adults. However, they do not passively accept people's existing preferences as between educational and non-educational uses of their time. On the contrary, these enthusiasts believe that if the adults they define as under-educated and disadvantaged really appreciated the benefits of further education to themselves and to others, then they would want the extra education for which they presently care so little. Once they had received the extra education they would want it.

This running debate over the development of adult education comprehends many of the major arguments for state intervention beyond the argument from externalities. The argument from externalities assumes that markets are sufficiently competitive to encourage human ingenuity and effort, and to act as a cheap and efficient method of control over the quality and quantity of educational services. Public intervention would then supplement the operation of these markets only in respect of external effects. In these scenarios, existing distributions of income and of values are a given. They are not a policy variable but part of the assumed-immutable circumstances within which education is provided. Other conditions, like ignorance among would-be learners, are simply assumed away. It is precisely to these circumstances and conditions that many of the non-externality arguments for public intervention refer.

Until quite recently the promotion of economic growth would have been widely advanced as a sound reason for public investment in the training of adults. However, there is nowadays a more widespread acceptance than there was in the sixties for the view that neither initial education nor continuing training can, of itself, have much effect on the rate of economic growth. Whatever the reasons for the exceptionally slow growth of the British economy since the Second World War, by international standards, it is widely believed that two important contributory factors have been the prevalence of attitudes hostile to industry — especially among highly educated adults — and a quite common indifference to the possibilities of technical progress. This is not to say that inadequacies in quality as well as quantity of initial and continuing education are unimportant. But they are probably symptom and consequence as well as cause of poor economic performance. The educational failure is nowhere clearer than in the prevailing values of so many educated adults, which is quite as important as underinvestment in new technologies. Indeed, the favourite American explanation of Britain's slow growth is that it stems from the country's culture and its social system. In the eighties, compared with the sixties, there is a certain scepticism about the growth yield on public investments in training. So training investments are generally assigned a more marginal role, for example the removal of skill bottlenecks, and greater attention is paid to public spending for equity purposes, e.g. on young people aged 16-24 years.

A great many non-externality reasons for public intervention have been advanced, but four of the most important are

- unwillingness to accept the consequences of the existing distribution of incomes;

- unwillingness to accept the consequences of the existing distribution of values;

- the need to remedy operational deficiencies in the private market for educational services;

- operational deficiencies in labour markets.

(1) Distribution of incomes

The supply of educational services will be skewed if it is exactly
geared to a demand which is entirely private, i. e. arising only from
the private decisions of households or firms. Under those circumstances firms buy-in only what they need for production reasons, and
households pay only for what they can afford. Both supply and demand
are skewed and limited by production exigencies and by the distribution
of household incomes.

Part of the moral appeal of the campaign for lifelong education has
come from its intention to remedy the most blatant inequalities of lifetime income and lifetime consumption profiles found in developed
countries. One consequence of existing income inequalities in these
countries is that private markets in educational services for adults work
better for the richer than for the poorer members of the community. To
those that have more is given. It is simply not feasible for low income
adults to forego earnings, risk security of employment or pay cost-
covering fees in order to undertake full-time education without employer
or public support. Zero or subsidised money prices and educational
entitlements are the only kind of public financial interventions available
to counteract the distributional consequences of income inequalities
until such time as inequalities of money income and wealth are directly
reduced.

(2) Distribution of values

If all money incomes were equalised overnight, people would purchase
and consume different quantities and qualities of educational services
with their equal incomes. If all services were provided at zero money
price, people would consume them in wildly varying quantities. They
would do so because tastes are not equally distributed among all adults.
One of the chief purposes of many forms of education is to influence the
formation of tastes and to change people's values. Economic analysis
often treats tastes as a given, a constant which is outside the analytical
framework. But for adult educators tastes are not a given. They are a
target variable. The community has always had a very strong interest
in promoting certain values and combating others by means of education.

Public intervention can be justified as a means of promoting society's
values. Intervention may be made necessary by the low value attached
to education by many adults. In initial education it is universal practice

in developed countries to compel attendance at school — although the
strict legal position, as in England and Wales, may be that parents must
ensure that children receive full-time education rather than attend
school. It is also common for governments to intervene in the school
curriculum, sometimes extensively. In some countries, and in varying
degrees, those with political power have convinced themselves that they
know better than children or parents what is educationally good for
children. The job of the state is to do to people whatever is educationally good for them, not to arrange for them to get what they want. At
first, people may not want what is good for them. D.H. Lawrence
wrote to his agent about the novel he had just finished, and how it
would be appreciated by the agent's young sons: 'My stuff is what they
want: when they know what they want. You wait.' (Lawrence, 1950,
pp. 53-54).

Looked at in this way, education is a 'merit good'. That is to say,
some people tend to undervalue its effects until they experience them,
after which they are supposed to feel that the element of compulsion is
justified. The state is thought to have a duty to promote education in
spite of any popular indifference or hostility. 'Government has the task
of creating merit wants' (Peston, 1981, p.542). It is even argued that
governments can fulfil another task which markets cannot possibly
perform: they can look after the interests of the unborn by educating
parents, employees and voters. Succeeding generations experience the
knock-on effects of contemporary education or the lack of it, but under
a market regime they cannot influence the allocation of resources to or
within education. 'The private approach to education fails to register
the social demand of future generations' (Miner, 1963, p.29).

Although the degree and kind of compulsion which is obvious in initial
education is rarer in post-initial education, a fundamental compulsion,
the compulsion to pay, is implicit in any use of taxation to finance
public expenditures on adult education. Value-preferences attributed to
the community are expressed by government through taxation, legislation,
subsidy and provision. Community preferences and private preferences
are not necessarily congruent, so adult education frequently has the
difficult task of serving two masters, the community and the individual.
As Prest (1975, p.68) pointed out, to put this double task on the political
process — enforcing 'correct' tastes and translating individual preferences into provision — requires 'a voting system which simultaneously
caters for the representation and the overriding of individuals'
preferences'.

(3) Deficiencies in educational markets

Educational services for adults are not always provided by public or
private suppliers competing keenly against each other to give the
customer what he or she wants as cheaply as possible. It frequently
happens that adults are in effect excluded, not by deliberate public
policy but

- by the insensitivity of suppliers to their needs;
- by the high non-money costs of informing themselves and
  arranging a contract between learner and teacher;
- by the virtual absence of any private capital market.

The first of these deficiencies, the insensitivity of suppliers and consequent alienation of many would-be learners, has many causes. One of
these is the fact that so many suppliers depend significantly on funding
from government or from sources other than the learner. The tendency
towards exclusivity in provision for adults has been explored by Alan
Thomas. He demonstrates the collective as well as the private loss
when, in a number of countries, facilities are not matched to the felt
needs of all groups but to 'those adults who are capable of translating
their needs into demands — broadly speaking, the already educated —
who enrol in existing or new programmes. Those who cannot articulate
their demands remain outside' (Thomas, 1981, p.189). The relative
failure of the Open University to reach the British working class started
from its capture at birth by the already-educated.

Another aspect of the same problem is the fact that less-educated,
poorer, socially disadvantaged people face higher information costs than
the more educated (see Bridge, 1978). Even if suppliers do not alienate
and are not intrinsically insensitive to the demands of non-participating
adults, they rarely spend the time and money which is necessary to
reduce for the least-educated the costs of acquiring, evaluating and
acting upon information about learning opportunities. High information
costs, together with inconvenient locations, inflexible scheduling, dis-
couraging admissions procedures and inappropriate instructional techniques constitute a formidable set of non-financial barriers, shutting out
many adults from the benefits of public spending.

Education, perhaps the best known example of human capital formation,
suffers from one of the most ineffective of all private capital markets.
Adults of slender means cannot offer enhanced future earnings as

collateral against which to borrow, in order to pay fees and maintain themselves during full-time education. They may be able to borrow against future earnings by mortgage, but only because a house is collateral. Since the capital of skills, knowledge and values is inalienable, it cannot serve as collateral and there is no way for the individual to capitalise the present value of a stream of expected earnings. Many adults of limited means are thrown back on the investment priorities of their employer — if they are fortunate enough to have one — or the benevolent instincts of the government — if it has any. For adults, in particular, it is still true 'that many first-rate abilities go forever uncultivated because no one, who can develop them, has had any special interest in doing so. This fact is very important practically, for its effects are cumulative' (Marshall, 1920, p. 550). Lack of education is one of the most damaging disadvantages from which an adult can suffer in modern society. It is cumulative because it is easily transmitted from parents to children, who then leave school at the earliest legal moment, or earlier, and continue the cycle of deprivation with their own children (see Groombridge, 1981). As a consequence of these difficulties, long-cycle adult education, as investment, depends heavily on employer financing or on public intervention by means of grants, loan schemes or the establishment of insurance-type funds.

Educational markets show a take-up of learning opportunities skewed towards the better-off. Low income adults are further disadvantaged because they are likely to have less initial education and higher information costs than higher income adults. Governments are lobbied to help low-income adults; but also to help adults rich and poor by creating financial mechanisms to assist self-investment in education which are alternative and even superior to a private capital market. This requires that governments go beyond helping people to convert future income into a present capital sum and provide help to those with poor-to-non-existent prospects of future earnings. Interventions to improve the operations of markets are often governed by efficiency considerations; but it is equity which argues for public investment in low income or otherwise disadvantaged adults or to improve the occupational mobility of risk groups in the working population.

(4) <u>Deficiencies in labour markets</u>

In the United Kingdom, economic growth is one of the preconditions for effective public interventions in adult education. Before and since Adam

Smith published An Inquiry into the Nature and Causes of the Wealth of Nations in 1776 economists have puzzled with only limited success over the causes of economic growth. In the sixties some people thought that education was one of the most important causes of economic growth. Since then professional opinion has swung towards the more cautious approach of many development economists. They usually regard certain kinds of educational investment as likely to increase the output of goods and services, if they can be combined with other policy actions in carefully specified circumstances.

If labour markets worked efficiently the private interests of employees and employers might ensure investment in the initial and continuing training of workers, by employees to enhance earnings and their job-getting capacity, by employers to enhance productivity and profits. But labour markets are not always so efficient. To what extent, if any, should such investment be paid for out of tax funds? For example, Hartley (1974, pp. 132-134) has argued for public intervention to counter under-investment in training, using a state manpower bank. Eventually state finance in the form of loans and grants would be supplied to individuals, including the unemployed and adults disadvantaged in other ways, to enable them to retrain, discover, inform themselves about, and move to new jobs. World Bank programmes are replete with examples of even more direct interventions in the form of public spending on adult literacy, agricultural extension and industrial training.

A strong case can often be made for what is really educational infrastructure spending on adults. Even in developed countries, with sophisticated capital markets and relatively abundant non-government capital resources, there is a case for public intervention if employees and employers appear to under-invest. Enterprises and employees pursuing their own interests may not invest sufficiently to improve the quality, and the geographical and occupational mobility, of the labour force. Sometimes the appropriate intervention takes the form of a compulsion on firms to allocate a proportion of cash flow to the continuing education of workers, as France does, because some firms are otherwise too limited or even myopic in their human capital formation (see Legave and Vignaud, 1979; Vincent, 1980). Sometimes public interventions are directed towards the re-entry of unemployed adults into productive employment. By the autumn of 1982 there were over 11 million adults registered as unemployed in the ten countries of the European Community. Without direct public intervention their chances of retraining and re-employment, already poor, would be far worse.

Labour markets in many countries work with only patchy efficiency to reallocate skills in response to structural changes in economies. Marginal interventions by governments in industrial training are often justified by civil servants as a means of overcoming skill shortages which might inhibit economic growth. In practice, it is difficult to be sure that it really is a skill shortage which is constraining growth, or that the cause of the skill shortage is under-training rather than under-utilisation of existing skills or geographical immobility of skilled workers.

Nevertheless, it is likely that underinvestment in new skills by firms or workers is sometimes a real and growth-inhibiting problem, for which some kind of public intervention, not necessarily public spending, is a solution. It is also true that such interventions are easier to finance when there is economic growth than when economies have stalled and public revenues are under severe pressure. There are many competing uses for tax funds and there are political limits on taxation levels. Over the last twenty years public spending as a proportion of gross domestic product has risen dramatically in Western European countries. In the smaller states like Belgium, Denmark, Holland and Sweden government spending now ranges between 50 and 65 per cent of GDP. It may not be accidental that in the biggest countries, like West Germany, France and the United Kingdom, after a sharp rise up to the mid-seventies, public spending seems to have reached a plateau at between 45 and 50 per cent of GDP.

GOVERNMENT INTERVENTIONS : METHODS

Actual interventions are even more difficult to reduce to order than the reasons given for intervening. Ad hocery is frequently the rule. Models of rational decision-making derived from neoclassical economics have only limited and occasional value as guides to the understanding of public interventions. Anthropological techniques provide useful insights (e. g. Heclo and Wildavsky, 1981). The Marxian model is in some respects even less useful than neoclassical economics. Like Christian theology or Freudianism, Marxism has a formidable capacity to construct post hoc explanations which fit into a universalistic explanation of behaviour. But it is not well adapted to provide precise guidelines or to generate appropriate information before a decision.

Neoclassical economics makes heroic assumptions about knowledge, rationality and the pursuit of efficiency which do not accord at all closely

Table 3:   State and private enterprise spending on training in France

	1973	1977 (3)
Trainees attending (1)		
State	956,000	894,000
Private enterprise	1,492,000	1,774,000
Training insurance funds	33,000	164,000
Total (2)	2,260,000	2,800,000
Trainee hours		
State	180,000,000	206,000,000
Private enterprise	103,000,000	101,000,000
Training insurance funds	2,090,000	12,000,000
Total	268,000,000	317,000,000
Budget, milliard FF		
State (4)	2.0	3.5
Private enterprise	3.7	7.5

(1)   Trainees on all or part of a course in the budget year.

(2)   Discrepancies between totals and the sum of the parts: some trainees benefit simultaneously from state and employer aid.

(3)   Provisional figures.

(4)   Initial appropriations only: in 1977 an additional appropriation of FF 1.63 milliard was allocated by budgetary amendment.

Source: Catherine Legave and Dominique Vignaud, Descriptions of Vocational Training Systems : France, European Centre for the Development of Vocational Training, Berlin, 1979.

with the reality of much government decision-making. One participant
observer has reported that '... in the government all information
regardless of its objective basis becomes political' and that '... the
degree to which an agency or branch of government attemtps to act as
if the "ideology of rational decision-making" actually has positive
utility is an increasing function of the degree to which it is politically
distant from the day-to-day operation of the program' (Stromsdorfer,
1979, p. 340). Neoclassical economics can provide a well-developed
taxonomy of decisions and their consequences, and several sets of
appropriate measures; but the selection of methods of intervention is
best understood in terms of values which are extra-economic.
Economic thinking influences some choices. But, more often, choices
of intervention technique arise out of rational responses by civil
servants and elected politicians to the structure of incentives which
each group faces. It is these incentives, or accident, or the unpredict-
able influence of political ideology, religion and culture which usually
provide the most plausible explanation.

The public sector of today is the residuary legatee of decades, and even
centuries, of ad hoc responses to crises of yesteryear. The result is a
system of financing peculiar to each country. A country like the
Netherlands had pluriformity written into its constitution as early as
1848, so that state and private provision are, as a general rule, on an
equal financial footing. Only 15 per cent of all vocational education is
organised by the state, the remainder being in the hands of (often
subsidised) denominational or ideological groups (see Baars, 1979). In a
country with different traditions, like France, state provision is more
important. Government subsidies for private enterprise provision (e. g.
measures for young people) and public earmarking of enterprise funds
for continuing training are of great and growing importance (see Table 3).

Evaluation of interventions

These country-specific financing habits, in which the state plays a varying role, require the raising of some funds through taxation. There are
examples of hypothecated taxes which are levied on firms, notably the
vocational training tax in France and contributions to an employer/
employee insurance-type fund in Norway. Otherwise, these tax revenues
involve direct welfare losses for the ordinary taxpayer. Income is
thereby redistributed from ordinary taxpayers to the beneficiaries of
educational services. One of the difficulties about financial interventions
which use general tax funds is that the taxation or the public spending or

the net effect of both may be regressive. That is to say, tax takes a decreasing proportion of income as income rises, or the net effect of taxing and spending favours the rich more than the poor.

It is part of the professional mythology of British educators that public spending favours the poor — hence the moral indignation of professionals at any reductions in public educational expenditures. The evidence is at best inconclusive. Much of it suggests that public educational spending favours the rich rather than the poor (see ACACE, 1982; Le Grand, 1982). Users of the Open University and of provision by the Responsible Bodies have been predominantly middle class, unless the analysis is rigged by determining the social class of a middle-aged adult from the social class of a parent. To increase tax funding of that kind of provision would probably increase rather than diminish social class inequalities in the take-up of educational opportunities.

In the United Kingdom, taxation based on ability to pay is not the general basis of taxation. In 1981 most taxation was regressive. Only 37.7 per cent of all tax revenues, from income and corporation taxes, were directly related to income (Lloyds Bank, 1982, Table 2). Even the income tax, which is the core of a progressive tax system, does not have a consistently progressive rate structure. One critic (Pond, 1982, pp. 55-56) summarises the position thus :

> 'The same marginal rate of tax (30p in the £ in 1980/81) is payable for a married wage earner on £45 a week (below the supplementary level) as by someone with the same family circumstances earning more than five times that amount. Indeed, if we take account of national insurance contributions, the marginal rate faced by those on £45 a week exceeds that payable on £250 a week. The only truly progressive element of the UK structure of tax rates are the higher rates of tax. Yet the higher rates now apply to only two in every hundred taxpayers. For the remaining 98 per cent of taxpayers, marginal rates of tax are higher for those at the bottom than for those at the top. '

Some experts estimate that in its entirety the British tax system is regressive for the lowest earners. The most favourable assessment is that it is mildly progressive for the poorest third of households. For the other two thirds of households the tax burden may be approximately proportional to income. However, over the whole range of household incomes, public spending, in so far as it can be attributed to individual households, tends to be regressive. Therefore, the net effect of taxing and spending is probably slightly regressive for most households. In choosing between financial and non-financial interventions, and between different types of intervention, an important criterion — using an ideology of rationality — should be their effect on the regressivity of the entire tax/spending regime.

Two programmes, one of adult retraining and the other the provision of recreational general education in Britain, can be considered in detail to illustrate the difficulties of matching the reality to the rhetoric of public intervention.

Even interventions to aid seriously disadvantaged adults, which are precisely targeted and totally tax funded, may not be very successful. This example draws very heavily on an excellent but somewhat depressing case study by Richard Berthoud (1978). He examined the training of men in craft skills at two government Skillcentres, in Stoke-on-Trent and in Dundee, over a three year period, including their success in local labour markets. Skillcentres try to help individuals to acquire a skill in order to improve job prospects; and they try to help industry by concentrating on supplying skilled men for occupations with skill shortages. After training and experience such men are expected to be treated like apprentice-trained men. On the open labour market workers and firms might realistically be expected to share between them the cost of training in these transferable skills. In some circumstances the worker might even bear the bulk of the cost burden. Trainable unemployed men may represent a failure of the market to finance an adequate supply of skills. Or they may represent an accurate estimate of industry needs by employers, which leaves would-be skilled men grossly under-equipped to compete for a secure and healthy income from employment. In order to remedy either or both of these conditions, British governments have intervened by subsidising other trainers, for instance with Key Training Grants, or by paying for and providing training, for instance in Skillcentres and Colleges of Further Education (see Table 4).

These courses vary greatly. In the seventies, three month office and clerical courses for women accounted for a large share of provision in colleges of further education. A two to three week Heavy Goods Vehicle course was the most common of those sponsored on employers' establishments. By contrast, Skillcentre courses were generally rather expensive six to twelve month courses for men, in engineering, electrical, mechanical and construction trades.

Table 4 :   Government skill training for adults in the United Kingdom

Courses	Completions	
	1970	1976
In colleges of further education	1,624	51,998
Sponsored in employers' establishments	201	14,241
Skillcentres	12,820	22,696
Other	882	720
	15,527	89,651

Source: R. Berthoud, Training Adults for Skilled Jobs: Skillcentre
training and local labour markets, Policy Studies Institute,
1978.

Berthoud (1978, p.46) concluded that the expected benefits to Skillcentre training could be classified as hedging: reduced risk of
unemployment; and increased wages when in work. Trainees from the
two Skillcentres in trade and non-trade jobs 'earned rather less in real
terms, after training than before'. Some 16 per cent were out of work
at the time of survey and another 43 per cent had taken work in non-
trade jobs in which they gained no benefits from their training. Moreover, these were only completees. It was not uncommon for 40 per cent
of starters to drop out from a course before completion. Immediately
after training, some 60 per cent of trainees found a first job 'in trade'
and just over 40 per cent were working in trade at survey time.
However, it has to be stressed that nearly one-third failed even to get
a start in trade and 60 per cent of those who did get a start in trade had
left those jobs and had mostly left the trade altogether by the time they
were surveyed, which was on average $1\frac{1}{2}$ years after completion.

Since the employment rate of trainees had improved slightly it was possible for Berthoud to conclude that, on balance, there was 'probably no loss in earning power, one man taken with another'. Set against high costs of training these are not impressive benefits, even if, on balance, improved job satisfaction could be added in. On the basis of the survey, nothing could be said about any improvement in social or geographical mobility as a result of change in status from unskilled to skilled.

Berthoud made a convincing case that difficulties in managing such training in the context of unmanaged labour markets were at the root of any failure. The proximate cause of the not very satisfactory post-training employment experience was weakness of demand for skilled labour. Before the great recession of the eighties, British employers tended to report big skill shortages in boom and still significant ones when demand was low. Unions had little effect on trainee recruitment. But the experience of trainees showed that their chances of getting into their trade were not good unless demand was really very high. The irony is that the attractiveness and effectiveness of such courses depends on getting into a trade. This in turn depends on completion co-inciding with a period of exceptional demand for skilled labour. Despite the grand talk which is sometimes heard about using training as a counter-cyclical measure, this is a very hard trick to accomplish. Output of trainees has to be cut back as demand improves, and down to a minimum as demand peaks, then increased as demand slackens and up to peak output as it bottoms. But opening and closing training facilities is not cheap and not like turning a tap. To fit the level of training activity to the business cycle requires an accuracy in forecasting magnitudes and timing which is simply not available. The only alternative is to try to train through a recession and stockpile skilled workers in non-trade jobs until high demand re-opens trade opportunities. Sadly, Berthoud (1978, p. 73) reports that this does not happen either.

Recreational general education for adults offers different lessons. It is not self-evident that such provision should always be provided or financed out of tax funds, nor that the present distribution of public spending is socially optimal. Social priorities change over time. Sections of the public budget which are non-competing when one political party controls central or local government become competing under another political regime. Sometimes, all political parties shift their priorities.

In England and Wales, Labour and Conservative administrations have moved in recent years to a new, bi-partisan policy with respect to the type of adult education which is provided mainly by Local Education Authorities and serves other than vocational needs. This policy has put a new emphasis on services to disadvantaged adults, at the expense of the more advantaged. The response of some of the professionals is to see 'a real danger that adult education may split into two segments : a heavily subsidised compensatory service for the conspicuously disadvantaged and an unsubsidised, and therefore highly priced, leisure service for the well-off' (Mee and Wiltshire, 1978, p.112). They hark back to the 'good old days' when this largely recreational kind of adult education was 'regarded as part of the public educational system to be maintained by public funds', with a fee so low it was little more than a registration fee. The fee did not contribute substantially towards costs, and it would not 'discourage the poorer members of the community from using the service' (Mee and Wiltshire, 1978, p.102). In similar vein, it is argued that non-professionals have misunderstood the recreational nature of this type of adult education. For successive governments to insist that it become largely self-financing 'is to deny the educational needs of much of the adult population : nothing is more calculated to turn the service into a middle-class preserve where only the popular and profitable activities survive' (ACACE, 1981, p.41).

Governments have to evaluate interventions in a more detached way than professionals in a given service. The government choice set is quite different from that of the professionals. Governments are unlikely to believe in financing adult education 'for its own sake'. In order to justify public subsidies the potential returns to society must first exceed the sum of the returns to private beneficiaries. If this is judged to be the case, the second test is to compare the social yield on this particular resource commitment, with its actual clientele, with the social yield on other possible uses for resources, non-educational as well as educational. Only if the commitment of public funds passes both tests is there a chance that subsidising this kind of adult learning will raise the level of educational investment and change its distribution from that which is privately-optimal to that which is socially-optimal.

In applying these tests, governments are likely to take into account the relatively unchanging social class composition of the clientele for this kind of education in the sixties and seventies (see ACACE, 1982, pp.50-51). Participation remains strongly biased towards younger, female adults drawn from the more educated and from the higher social classes.

A survey in 1968, when fee-financing was negligible, showed women out-numbering men by more than three to one, the elderly greatly under-represented, the more educated greatly over-represented. The nominal fees of the old regime were supposed not to discourage the 'poorer members of the community'. They were certainly discouraged by something. Adult students in the top three social classes out-numbered those in the other three social classes by three to one, although the top three constituted one third of the population sample and the other three two thirds (NIA E, 1970).

A policy switch from negligible to largely fee-financing of recreational education could hardly convert into a middle class preserve what was already one. Labour and Conservative administrations decided to force the ever-growing British middle class to make a much larger direct contribution from household income for a consumer-durable type of education. Tax funds would then be released for non-educational purposes, or concentrated on adult literacy tuition and other compensatory education and training programmes which could not possibly be financed through the market from household disposable incomes. Governments are unlikely to share the disdain of some professionals for the survival of 'only the popular and profitable activities' in a field of provision where so much of the benefit is private and so many beneficiaries have already demonstrated their willingness to pay for these private benefits. The rate fund revenue account of local authorities in England and Wales 1974/75 to 1979/80 (Local Government Financial Statistics, 1978, Table 7; 1981, Table 9) shows a marked swith over great tracts of post-school institutionalised education from tax financing towards user charging. The proportion of all educational spending which was raised from user charges approximately doubled, from 3 to 6 per cent. But in the post-school institutions used by adult learners (non-advanced and advanced further education and adult education institutes) user charges were by 1979/80 commonly providing 15 to 25 per cent of all funds instead of 5 to 15 per cent in 1974/75. During these same years government was increasing tax financing of learning opportunities for seriously disadvantaged adults, e.g. through specific grants, as for the adult literacy campaign, and through the Manpower Services Commission's Training Opportunities Scheme.

This entire episode offers a clear example of a change in public policy based on a threefold government judgement

  - about priorities in public spending;

- about the appropriateness of particular methods of raising funds to one type of education;

- and about the nature and incidence of benefits from that education.

The dramatic cut in the level of public subsidy enjoyed by some adults was based partly on a correct estimate that there would not be a reduction in participation proportionate to the subsidy reduction, and partly on government determination to make public spending on adult education more progressive by switching it from the advantaged to the disadvantaged.

What is probably a once and for all substitution of household funds for tax funds has now occurred in the financing of recreational adult education. The correct response to any fee-induced narrowing of the social class composition of the clientele which might occur is to reverse it through financial support for poorer adults — if such a narrowing conflicts with public policy objectives. To an extent this already happens. Such discrimination is opposed by institutions who are fighting to retain control of what is learned by whom, against the threat of fee-paying customers who suddenly have the institution's life in their hands.

The evaluation of Skillcentre training and of liberal or general education illustrate the difficult judgements which must be made by governments. In OECD countries much money has been spent trying to discover whether the kind of social engineering exemplified by many public interventions in educational provision makes any difference, and, if so, what that difference is (e.g. Fagerlind, 1975; Jencks, 1979). Experimental designs for the evaluation of public spending on education are ruled out as unethical or politically unfeasible. Evaluations carried out after the event are a difficult, almost heroic enterprise, whose product does not command widespread credibility. Nevertheless, the evaluative effort and the interventions have to continue. As Stromsdorfer (1979, p.345) points out, it is spurious to argue that one should not tinker with the lives and fortunes of individuals, because this involves arguing that random tinkering is better than purposive tinkering.

Methods and instruments of public intervention

The methods used to raise and to spend funds, are, in effect, instruments of public intervention in the financial system of a country. They have substantial and manifold repercussions. Governments have two principal ways of raising funds: taxation and borrowing. The choice between the two methods is important because the consequences of taxing are not at all the same as the consequences of borrowing. The consequences of borrowing vary according to the level of economic activity, the demands of other borrowers, and the propensity of households and enterprises to save. There are circumstances in which the use of one method of raising funds rather than the other tends to push up the price level, and other circumstances in which it tends to depress production of goods and services. Nor are the distributional effects of taxation and borrowing the same: they impact on different groups of the population in different ways.

There are also two principal ways in which governments spend funds. The policy choice between them is generally as neglected by educationists as the policy choice between ways of raising funds. Governments spend funds (1) to purchase resources in order to provide educational services direct, or (2) by transferring funds to non-government suppliers of services or to adult learners for them to spend. In the choice between direct provision and transfer there is a wide variation in practice between developed countries, and in the same country over long periods of time. In the United Kingdom it is now normal for just over one half of central and local government spending — for all purposes — to be devoted to provision, the rest taking the form of transfer payments like subsidies, loans, pensions, and interest payments. Because of an abysmal lack of published financial data, it is difficult even to guess at what should be known: the ratio in adult education between direct government provision and government transfer payments. Such data are necessary if there is to be informed public choice between each regime (provision or transfer) with its consequences for the quality, quantity and distribution of learning opportunities for adults.

Financing arrangements are one of the prime determinants of the distribution of educational benefits between individuals. Indeed, it is desirable to include in the information base for public decisions not only data on spending on educational provision and transfers, but also public spending on non-educational transfers which might easily be transmuted into education-specific transfers or funds for direct educational provision. Cash benefits paid to the unemployed are a case in point. By 1981/82 the Manpower Services Commission was spending £85 million a year (MSC 1982, p.19) on 25,000 places in an expanding Community Enterprise Programme to fund co-operatives and training workshops for both the young unemployed and for the long-term older unemployed.

In a quiet way, the British government was recognising that the unemployed were bound to be expensive, so that there is a case for using
'dole' money — non-educational transfer payments — to subsidise
employers who are willing to give people a chance to learn, a chance to
gain a good reference and a chance to earn through work.

Apart from methods of raising funds, five important types of intervention instrument can be listed:

(1)   direct cash payments from central or local government to public
      or private suppliers of educational services for adults. In
      ascending order of public commitment, these transfers to institu-
      tions take the form of below-economic cost loans, revenue
      deficiency grants, and grants to cover the total cost of provision.
      The intention and effect is to increase the availability of benefits-
      in-kind at low or zero money prices.

(2)   cash transfers from government to adult learners. The first
      class of intervention instruments transfer tax funds to sellers of
      services. This second class transfer funds to buyers, in the form
      of subsidised study loans, outright grants or variations on tied
      purchasing power such as entitlements or drawing rights. The
      first class will reduce money prices and/or increase supply; the
      second increases demand at existing prices.

(3)   tax concessions or tax exemptions — sometimes called 'tax
      expenditures' — which have an effect equivalent to a public subsidy
      but involve no accounted cash outlay. These concessions are made
      to institutions, e.g. educational charities in the United Kingdom,
      or to buyers, e.g. allowances for private educational expenditures
      set against income tax.

(4)   control of money prices, beyond that exercised through (1), in
      order to lower or eliminate fees.

(5)   rules for officials or for transactors relating to the financing and
      offer of educational services, e.g. budgetary constraints and
      incentives, rules concerning scheduling and location of instructional
      services. These rules seek to influence the budgetary decisions of
      those who supply educational services, including decisions about the
      nature of the provision being financed out of budgets, for instance
      quotas on participants and prohibitions on particular uses of public
      funds.

Systematic consideration of experience with so wide a range of instruments, deployed in different circumstances from country to country,
would fill several books. Sufficient here to note briefly a few features
of the way in which these instruments are deployed.

The five classes of instrument are not simply interchangeable in theory
or in practice. In practice, their effects on the behaviour of people and
organisations vary so much that the possibility of substituting one class
of instrument for another can be quite limited. In economic theory,
strong grounds for state intervention by regulation — such as the high
information costs faced by some adults — are not equally strong grounds
for state ownership of facilities. Enforcement of minimum standards of
provision and of accuracy in advertising are easily justified from
differential information costs, as is public spending on the dissemination
of information and on counselling. Education with large external
benefits may be increased by extra funding from tax revenues. But to
achieve the desired outcome it is not essential that public funds be used
in publicly-owned rather than privately-owned institutions. Ownership
is nothing like as important as control.

In many of the larger OECD countries direct government provision of
adult education is less important than public subsidies for private sector
provision or regulation of unsubsidised private sector provision,
especially provision by firms. For a long time, many OECD governments have directly provided post-school initial education or they have
heavily subsidised non-government provision. But the preferred
methods of institutional finance have consistently favoured direct transfer from schools into consecutive full-time education, while deterring
or inhibiting postponement of education into later adult life. Direct
government involvement in post-initial education has been heaviest in
programmes aimed at the youngest adult unemployed, at skill shortages
and at easing the pains of structural and technological change in an
economy. Some countries, like Sweden and the United States (see
Woodhall, 1982), have well-developed state guaranteed and subsidised
loan schemes directed towards the learner. But for the most part
governments have preferred to finance central and local government
institutions, non-government organisations and employers. It may be
that there is a long-run trend towards a substitution of tax finance for
user charging, partly in pursuit of allocative efficiency, partly on
equity grounds. If so, it is a hesitant trend, and the pros and cons of
tax versus price financing are much debated (e. g. Mushkin, 1972;
Bird, 1976; Seldon, 1977; Foster, 1980; Prest, 1982).

Among some of the professional adult educators there has been intense discussion of interventions designed to increase the power of learners while diminishing the power of institutions (see Michaelson, 1978). One highly favoured device is the educational entitlement, which is from the same family as educational vouchers and educational drawing rights (see Kurland, 1977; Edding, 1981; ACACE, 1982). The general absence of such entitlements should be seen in perspective. It has been pointed out (Glennerster, 1981, p. 556) that strong tax incentives and compulsory contributions from earnings are commonly used to force workers to save and invest for retirement. But, apart from rare exceptions like the Norwegian insurance-type scheme for financing industrial training, no comparable state incentives or compulsions exist to encourage workers to save and invest in training or general education throughout their working lives.

Tax relief is used widely and on a large scale to encourage another socially approved activity, home ownership. In June 1982 the British housing pressure group, Shelter, estimated that the British government foregoes £1,985 million in tax revenues each year in order to encourage home ownership. This is equivalent to an average annual public subsidy of £327 to each mortgage holder. Technically, this is a tax expenditure, and as such it is broadly equivalent in effect to a cash transfer to the activity which is being encouraged. Tax expenditures in the form of tax allowances on educational expenditures by adults are potentially an important means of enhancing the educational autonomy of tax-paying adult learners (see Leslie, 1978), although their potential has so far been little used. Bendick (1977, Table 5-9) estimates that in 1970 in the United States, all forms of tax expenditures, in aid of institutions as well as individual taxpayers, accounted for a mere 2.7 per cent of implicit and explicit revenues for all systematic instruction, against 51.8 per cent for the value of student time and 34.7 per cent for explicit government expenditures.

CHAPTER FOUR: THE PRIVATE SECTOR: PARAFISCS, ENTERPRISES, HOUSEHOLDS

PARAFISCS

The private sector includes three of the sectors in the four sector model of the adult education industry. These three, parafiscs, enterprises and households, are the non-government entities engaged in financing and resourcing adult learning opportunities. The parafiscal sector is an umbrella classification for a collection of organisations which are heterogeneous but have certain distinctive characteristics in common. The distinguishing features of parafiscal organisations are (1) their sources of finance, and (2) the output which is being financed.

The financing and output characteristics of parafiscs are interdependent, but in ways which are by no means fully understood. Many parafiscs provide some of the same kind of collective consumption services for adults as tax-financed government institutions. For example, in England the Royal College of Surgeons carries out research, advanced training and certification functions which are similar in many, but not all respects to the activities of tax-financed university medical schools. However, the College is quite differently constituted and financed. University medical schools are funded almost exclusively by grants from the University Grants Committee, channelling tax funds to universities, and by grants from the National Health Service and from the Medical Research Council, which also come out of the tax revenues. At the end of the 1970s the Royal College of Surgeons of England was spending and receiving in income almost £1.6 million a year (see figure 4, page 66). In addition to its wide-ranging research activities, the College has a programme of education and training in surgery, dental surgery and anaesthetics, and in standards of practice and patient care. The origins of this independent voluntary non-profit organisation go back six hundred years to the Guild of Surgeons in the City of London. In 1800 it was given a royal charter to exercise legal control over the initial and continuing training of surgeons, and in 1953 the College was registered as a charity with the objects defined in its charter of 1800. It claims that it 'exists for the benefit of the whole community' and that 'it is precluded from acting for the professional advantage of its own Fellows unless this is identical with the interests of the community' (Royal College of Surgeons).

Figure 4:   Income and Expenditure of the Royal College of Surgeons of England

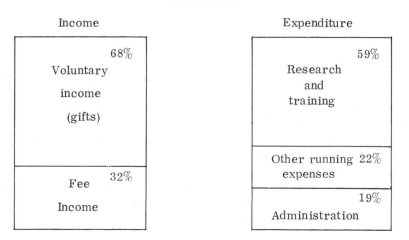

Income   Expenditure

Source: Royal College of Surgeons of England, Into the Eighties.

If, as the College suggests, the benefits of its activities spill over generously to the community at large, some financial support might be expected to come from that community.   Otherwise there would be comprehensive free riding by non-members.   Only one third of the College's income is market-based, i.e. fees for services and the sub-scriptions of approximately 15,600 Fellows.   The remaining two thirds of the College's income comes in the form of donations, grants, covenants, legacies, interest-free loans and endowments.   Tax allow-ances can be important in this kind of financing.   Gifts of securities and other assets can be made, free of liability to Capital Gains Tax or Capital Transfer Tax on the part of the donor or the College. A legacy is free from Capital Transfer Tax up to the prevailing limit for all charitable gifts on death.   Single donations, in the form of a Deposited Covenant, and an annually covenanted gift from taxed income by individuals or partnerships allow the College to reclaim the donor's Income Tax at the current basic rate.   In the case of a donor company, the cost to the donor can be reduced by setting all its covenanted pay-ments against Corporation Tax.

These tax concessions mean that, in addition to the value of the gifts received, the College receives from the government the basic rate tax

which has been paid on covenanted individual or partnership income.
For example, if someone covenants to pay £25 a year to the College,
the income tax recoverable by the College is another £10.75, assuming
that income tax is paid at a basic rate of 30 per cent. So the general
taxpayer has to increase the total value of the gift from £25 to £35.75
a year. It is the general taxpayer who increases the sum, because the
effect of the concession is to erode the yield from taxation. For every
erosion of yield there must be a compensating reduction somewhere in
public spending, or an increase in government borrowing or taxation.
The £10.75 cash payment is an explicit subsidy directed to be paid out
of public funds by the donor-taxpayer at the expense of the general
taxpayer. It is not a government-directed subsidy, except that the
object of the subsidy, the College, is a legally recognised object for
such gifts. It is the donor-taxpayer who decides whether a public
subsidy shall be paid, how large it is to be, and to which recognised
charity it should go. By contrast, reliefs from Capital Gains and
Capital Transfer taxation are implicit subsidies, tax expenditures,
which effectively increase the income of the College by stimulating a
level of donations in excess of the yield to an organisation lacking
charitable status. But any gain to the College is not achieved by cash
transfer from tax funds to the College. For example, the relief on
company donations operates only in so far as it encourages company
generosity. If this happens, the yield of Corporation tax is eroded;
but the revenue of the College is not improved beyond the value of the
donations.

The output: funding relationship

Peston (1972, p. 33) has argued that 'the ability of a voluntary body to
provide a public good may depend on its ability to supply a private good
jointly with it. People will then join the organisation for the sake of the
private benefits and in doing so be charged for a share of the public good
too'. Where the public or collective good element in the parafisc's output is minor, relative to the private good element, this may sometimes
be the case. But the Royal College of Surgeons is representative of a
type of parafisc in which the collective good component is dominant. It
is possible, as Weisbrod suggests, that the share of collective good
output in the private plus collective good output of a parafisc is roughly
proportional to the share of voluntary income in its total income. With
his customary pragmatism, Peston (1972, p. 33), feeling that voluntary
provision of a collective good could not be regarded as irrational,
simply remarks that it 'appears not to fit very well into mainstream

economic reasoning'. Such behaviour seems to depend on altruism rather than the normal selfishness assumption used by neoclassical economists. With the aid of the new economics of public choice (see Mueller, 1979) and other cross-disciplinary analyses, American economists like Burton Weisbrod have continued the struggle to make sense of the behaviour of those who finance parafiscs and those who decide the character of their output.

The private provision of collective goods need not depend on altruism. Governments, with their power to compel payment, can overcome the free rider behaviour and correct the allocative failures of private markets. But there is a solution which does not rely on compulsion. This requires an institutional means of expressing the private demands of subgroups in the population for goods which have large spillovers and are undersupplied by government — which is itself subject to allocative failure.

Weisbrod (1977, p. 71) has pointed out that economic analysis, obsessed by the example of government spending on defence, has concentrated too heavily on one of the characteristics attributed to collective goods: their quantity is supplied equally and inescapably to all consumers. Weisbrod argues that inadequate attention is paid to the inequality in demands for such goods, and to the inequality in the extent of benefits between individuals. For him the crucial characteristic of a collective consumption good is not its technical availability to many people simultaneously, but the number of simultaneous beneficiaries, people whose private wants are differentially satisfied by the good. Indeed, a collective good which satisfies a private want for some people may be most unwelcome to others, so various are private responses to a given service.

Applying Weisbrod's insights, it can be seen that subgroups of the whole population may come to the distinctly non-altruistic conclusion that it is worthwhile for them to finance provision some of which meets directly their individual needs, some of which spills over in an uncontrolled and unchargeable fashion but only within the subgroup, some of which spills over outside the group of subscribers. Cross-subsidy of the provision of collective goods out of market-based revenues is usually only feasible where those revenues are a large part of total revenue and collective goods a small part of total output. Weisbrod's earlier work (1964) demonstrated the complexity of such spillovers in the case of public education. Spillovers beyond the subscribing group may well be tolerated where they arise from a collective good output which is unavoidable joint-product with private good output. No altruism is involved. In other cases, households or firms which might fund parafiscs have only to decide whether, on balance, the net benefits likely to accrue to them exceed those available from an alternative employment of the same sum of money.

It is necessary to formulate and test hypotheses about parafiscal financing and output behaviour against aggregative data, but also to study individual cases in order to generate hypotheses. Economists often model a market as a bargaining, allocative and signalling mechanism which caters for anonymous, undifferentiated buyers and sellers. But the reality of the education industry is very different. There are many collectives, such as parafiscs and enterprises, which are less comprehensive than the state. They engage in market operations and respond, to a certain extent, to market forces. But they do not behave like the single-minded maximisers of profit (sellers) or of private satisfactions (buyers) who are assumed to operate the price system in the model market. Many parafiscs supply collective-type goods in a way which no well-bred creature of the model market would ever do. Their marketed services are of two kinds. For some, members pay a market price to enjoy private benefits, and this takes the form of a subscription. Other services, for non-members as well as members, are individually priced. Like the government, the parafisc may supply services with separable benefits at prices ranging up to cost-covering ones. On the one hand the parafisc is supplying collective goods for free; on the other it is often selling services alongside government and for-profit educational institutions.

The educational activities of professions and trades unions, churches, charities and political parties can be quantitatively significant. Maureen Woodhall (1977) estimated that in 1970 in the United Kingdom about 17 per cent of all spending on post-initial education and training of adults was devoted to professional training, and the parafiscal organisations of the professions have a powerful role in this continuing education. For many kinds of parafisc educational activities are subsidiary to the group's main purpose. Other parafiscs are essentially an educational or cultural mission, for example, in Britain, the Workers' Educational Association or the Royal Academy of Arts. Self-governed by artists, the Royal Academy was founded in 1768 to provide England's first art schools and to exhibit the work of living artists. It still has a unique position in art education in Britain. Its annual turnover is £20 million.

Its income comes chiefly from tuition fees, admission charges and sponsorship. One million people visit its galleries each year. It has 30,000 'Friends' and in 1982 received gifts of capital worth £1.6 million from friendly individuals and firms and £250,000 from the government.

Until recently, the behaviour of voluntary non-profit organisations, with multiple sources of funding, has not been subjected to the kind of scrutiny accorded to the behaviour of enterprises or government. Theoretical and empirical work has so far tended to concentrate on distinguishing their characteristic outputs and mode of financing, with particular emphasis on the mix of outputs and the mix of revenue sources (see Weisbrod, 1977; Clement, 1979).

Output characteristics

The output criterion for a standard parafiscal organisation seems to be a profile of outputs which includes private goods, purchased indirectly by subscription or directly by fees; and collective goods, cross-subsidised out of market-based revenues or financed out of cash or in-kind public and private donations. Free rider behaviour may have an inhibiting effect on some potential funders. But educational parafiscs nevertheless manage to provide a very wide range of educational and cultural services which either add to or complement a similar output of partial collective goods by the public sector. Government-funded or government-provided institutions are not the only or even the most efficient way of providing partial collective goods. The pathology of government, no less than the pathology of markets, breeds a cautious pragmatism about the selection of institutional means for achieving the goals of public policy.

Weisbrod (1977, p. 61) has suggested that the size of the voluntary sector, relative to the public (compulsory non-profit) sector, can be expected to be a function of the heterogeneity of demands from the population. The burgeoning literature of the economics of public choice has illuminated not only the characteristics of market failure, but also the difficulties of using the majority rule political process to determine the correct tax-price when the quantities and qualities of educational services being demanded vary as much as they do between taxed adults. Even a partial collective good is supposed to be one which, if not supplied equally to all consumers, is at least supplied to many simultaneous beneficiaries. The problem with education is that the same service may have profound disutility for some taxpayers — and not just deschoolers; may be regarded with total indifference by others; and may be perceived as mildly-to-vastly beneficial by another segment of the adult population. Weisbrod has suggested that the more similar are the quantities and qualities demanded by consumers at a given set of tax-prices the less will be the undersatisfied demand at those prices, and the smaller will be the size of the voluntary sector relative to the government sector. Conversely, the more heterogeneous is the demand among taxpayers, the greater will be the share of the voluntary sector in the provision of educational services with collective good characteristics.

Nor will the collective-type goods supplied by parafiscs necessarily replicate those provided by public authorities. Weisbrod has made the interesting suggestion that one way of characterising the distinctive outputs of the voluntary sector is as collective goods demanded by a minority of the citizenry:

> 'Often these minorities consist of those persons in the population with qualitatively different tastes from the majority as in the case of adherents to minority religions. In a rapidly changing world, however, minorities may also include those groups demanding goods that the median voter will later learn to demand. In an era of social change, the voluntary sector may pioneer new collective goods that later become outputs of the government sector' (Weisbrod, 1977, p. 119).

Under certain assumptions, it is even predicted (Weisbrod, 1977, p. 67) that 'if two political units (such as countries) differ in the degree of heterogeneity of the populations, the more homogeneous unit will, ceteris paribus, have a lower level of voluntary-sector provision of collective-type goods or their private good substitutes'. But it is not yet known how much evidence there is outside the United States to support this hypothesis, or Weisbrod's rider (1977, pp. 2-3) that the voluntary non-profit institutions provide more of the same type of services that the compulsory non-profit sector provides, whereas for-profit private institutions provide services which are different in kind, i. e. private rather than collective-type goods. It is clear that conditions are rarely equal between political units. Moreover, educational history shows that parafiscs are highly innovatory suppliers. Sometimes they pioneer for the public sector. But they may also provide services for which the median voter never acquires so strong a taste that he is prepared to take provision completely into the public sector.

Funding characteristics

It could be argued that the revenue criterion for the standard parafisc should be heterogeneity of sourcing. In Chapter Two these sources were classified into government aid, direct subscription or donation revenue, and sales revenue. In one dimension, the essence of this heterogeneity is a mixing of tax-based and market-based revenue with funds which are not government subsidy and do not reflect a quid pro quo of the kind which is implicit in user charges and in subscriptions. In another dimension, this heterogeneity consists of a mixing of money and non-money forms of support. Money support may take the form of cash subsidies from government, sales revenue, subscriptions and donations from households and firms. Non-money support means (1) goods and services provided for the parafisc at zero or below-cost money price by government, firms or households, and (2) tax concessions.

One of Weisbrod's principal hypotheses concerns the determinants of public and voluntary sector shares in the financing of collective-type goods. However, there are other important features of the relation-ship between parafiscal financing and behaviour which require investigation. Modes of financing can be conceived as a continuum, with pure tax-financing as one pole and pure for-profit price-financing as the other. Parafiscal institutions might be arranged along this continuum according to their reliance on taxes or on for-profit sales revenue. Towards the tax pole are non-standard parafiscs, single function statutory bodies such as the Fonds d'Assurance Formation (FAF) in France and the AER in Denmark.

By mid-1979 there were 85 Training Insurance Funds (FAF), covering over 64,000 enterprises and 3 million employees. They are only one of five (not mutually exclusive) options which are available to those French employers with a legal obligation to participate in the financing of continuing vocational training (see Vincent, 1980, pp. 32-44). In 1976 some 10 million of France's 17.6 million employees worked in firms which were subject to this obligatory participation (Legave and Vignaud, 1979, p. 79). One of the defining characteristics of these funds, under the law of July 16, 1971, is that they are exclusively intended to finance training costs, whether the money is used for wage-earners or for the self-employed. Though the training funds are administered on a parity basis by employers and trades unions, they are financed out of contribu-tions from employers or the self-employed and not from employees.

Their function is strictly defined by law and by each fund's founding agreement between employers and unions. Their financing is essentially from a single source: the cash flow of enterprises. Legave and Vignaud (1979, p. 77) insist that 'the obligatory participation in financing continuing training is neither a tax nor any kind of official levy: it is merely an obligation to allocate funds into training'. While the spending options available to employers make the scale of employer contributions to the training funds uncertain, the statutory basis of the mandatory assignment of company cash to training leads others to the conclusion that the training funds do depend, for practical purposes, on a special kind of tax. Taxes which are avoidable, in this case by spending money on training in another way, are still taxes. In Denmark, the Arbejdsgivernes Elevrefusian is a nation-wide statutory agency, also a single function body and raising funds exclusively from employers by levy.

Institutions like the FAF and the AER have their activities and financing so circumscribed, by law or collective agreement, that their constitutions can look closer to that of a voluntary employers' consortium or a government agency than to a standard parafisc. At the end of the spectrum opposite to the tax pole are other institutions, in a grey area between unambiguously non-profit voluntary organisations and for-profit price-financed organisations. A case in point is the Escuela Profesional Politecnica at Mondragon in Spain.

Within fifty miles of Mondragon there is a dynamic and highly disciplined community of 123 co-operatives. At the centre of this unique organisation is the Caja Laboral Popular. This is a Co-operative Savings Bank, but at the same time an investment bank specialising exclusively, through its Empresarial (Managerial) Division, in the investment of Basque savings in the Mondragon Co-operatives. By 1978 the turnover of these Co-operatives exceeded £200 million a year and the labour force numbered about 14,000.

The Escuela Profesional Politecnica was the original foundation (1943) of the Mondragon Co-operatives. It is a Co-operative Polytechnic. In 1978, in addition to 1,300 students aged 15 and over, and another 800 studying languages, it had 600 mature students. It is structured as a co-operative, and is closely associated with a Student Producer Co-operative (Alecoop) where students can earn money to pay their fees and support themselves during their studies. Nearly all of the 600 mature students work in Alecoop (see Royal Arsenal, 1979, p. 34) :

- it offers work experience similar to work in other producer
  co-operatives;

- it works co-operatively and offers experience of that;

- students can earn enough to provide substantial maintenance in
  addition to paying their tuition fees; in 1978 they averaged
  15,000 pesetas or £100 per month.

In 1978 college revenues totalled 100 million pesetas, approximately
£690,000. In a country where state provision for technical training for
workers was generally very poor, the Basque Co-operatives had to find
an alternative to tax-financed technical education. The solution was to
finance technical education out of student fees and enterprise contributions. Although a government subsidy now provides almost one fifth of
total college revenue, two fifths comes from fees and other college-
generated income, and two fifths from enterprise contributions (Table 5).
The sourcing of the college is as varied as almost any parafisc which
can be found. Moreover, there is an explicit connexion between some
of these revenues and college outputs. The one third of college income
which is drawn from other co-operatives comes out of the 10 per cent
of their profits which these other co-operatives are obliged to allocate
to educational and social purposes under their constitutions. This high
level of community commitment to the college arises from the high
proportion of benefits which spillover to the Co-operatives and into the
general prosperity of the Basque country. The college provides workers
for the Co-operatives who are equipped not only with appropriate technical skills but with the co-operative ethic. Seventy per cent of the
executives of the Mondragon Co-operatives have graduated from the
College (Royal Arsenal, 1979, p.33).

To become a member of, that is to work in, a Co-operative, requires
a minimum capital investment of 250,000 pesetas, say £1,700. Trade
unions had no part in establishing Mondragon, and still have no part.
The Co-operatives are associations of capitalists, but capitalists whose
corporate and individual investments in education aim at more than the
creation of skills. Regional development, a work ethic and a concept of
an equitable distribution of earnings are also fundamental objectives,
'Saving in Mondragon means jobs in Mondragon' (Royal Arsenal, 1979,
p.12). It is this community interest which leads the Basques to save
and invest through the Caja Laboral Popular, not interest rates on
savings, and certainly not the rule that the highest wage must never
exceed the lowest by a factor of more than three.

Table 5:   Revenues of Escuela Profesional Politecnica, 1978

Source	% of total revenue
Contributions from ULARCO and AMAT Co-Operatives	35
Contributions from firms other than Co-operatives	5
Student fees	32
Income generated by college (research etc.)	10
Ministry of Education grant	18
	100

Source: Royal Arsenal Co-Operative Society, Mondragon: The Basque
Co-Operatives, 1979, p.35

The college output shows that it is not merely a group training centre
working for a consortium of enterprises which happen to be co-operatives,
and cleverly financed more from student fees and government subsidy
than from enterprise funds. The payment of fees by students signifies
acceptance of the principle of joint but personal financial participation
by workers in human as well as physical capital formation. The
importance of the contributions from the Co-Operatives is that they
testify to a fundamental commitment to the educational and cultural
development of the community.

Not all the output of the college returns to the contributing Co-Operatives.
But there is a group cohesion which is the key to the financing of the
college. The theoretical argument for the 3:1 ratio between top and
bottom wages 'is simply that a co-operative's wages policy must take
account of the need for group cohesion as well as of market constraints'
(Oakeshott, 1978, p.53). The rule allocating 10 per cent of profits to
social and educational projects in the locality serves to reinforce this
cohesion. It pays to invest in group cohesion. Nearly all the loan capital
needed by the Co-Operatives is raised in the local community by the Caja

Laboral Popular. A securely-financed set of industrial co-operatives, and the would-be co-operators who are also mature students and members of Alecoop, all see the advantages of a joint corporate and personal investment in education.

At opposite ends of the parafiscal spectrum, the Fonds d'Assurance Formation and the Escuela Profesional Politecnica might be regarded as limiting cases. The FAF have a form of financing which is only technically non-tax funding, management by the social partners, and very little freedom of manoeuvre with respect to goals or funding. The Escuela Profesional Politecnica has much more diversified funding, varied outputs, but a degree of subordination to a group of industrial enterprises. Neither organisation is government-owned and financed out of general taxation, nor for-profit and price-financed; but neither fits comfortably into the description of a voluntary non-profit organisation. Such institutions demonstrate the degree of simplification which is implied by any simple tripartite classification into tax-based, parafiscal and for-profit organisations. As Weisbrod (1977, p.173) recognised, a simple collectiveness index such as the ratio of gift revenue to total revenue provides only a one-dimensional measure for a very heterogeneous collection of organisations. Both the FAF and the Escuela Profesional Politecnica provide collective-type goods most of whose spillovers benefit a select group of the adult population and a select group of firms. These enterprises provide some or all of the funds, and the organisations might be regarded as the captives of the firms and the workers.

Government aid?

A further caveat should be entered. Not everyone thinks that organisations which are undoubted parafiscs should be given the public financial assistance, in money or non-money form, which they often receive. Though it is not his own position, Edding (1981, p.125) has pointed out that a case can be made that parafiscs, like firms, are acting primarily in their own interest, i.e. that of members, of donors or of those who pay any fees which they may charge. Occupational groups, chambers of commerce, churches and political parties want to ensure group loyalty and public reputation. Government financial assistance is not obviously necessary in all cases. The parafiscs may produce some collective-type goods; but these may be demanded exclusively by a tiny minority of adults. That case is sometimes countered with specific examples where public goals are achieved at very low public financial cost. But the argument for unselective public financial aid may not seem decisive.

In some countries, such as France, trade unions have had some success, through leverage on governments and employers, in improving the availability of learning opportunities for adults. As collectives, unions are not devoted primarily to the good of non-members. It has been argued (e.g. West, 1981, p.581) that, to the extent that they succeed in earmarking an increased share of company cash flow or of tax funds for the private benefit of union members, to that extent they help bring about a perverse distribution of income, i.e. one which is at the expense of the poorest and least organised members of the community.

There are market conditions under which some or all of any increase in training costs incurred by firms can be passed on to the consumers of the firm's products or to all the firm's employees. Government contributions to parafiscs are actually taxpayer contributions. Since the tax systems in a number of OECD countries are arguably regressive at the margin, the net effect of extra funding of parafiscs by firms and governments can be a more perverse distribution of incomes. The counter-argument is that this is a typically conservative, blocking defence, that improvements usually have to be piecemeal, and that the solution is to tackle perverse distributions and not to hinder educational initiatives. Nevertheless, it is necessary to monitor the institutional development of continuing education for the tendency to advance the learning prospects of some groups, like the male salariat, while paying far less attention to adults who are unemployed, retired or female. Not all subgroups of the adult population are equally competent and well-placed to promote their group interests through voluntary non-profit organisations.

ENTERPRISES

The for-profit segment of the private sector comprises two quite different kinds of for-profit enterprise. One kind is the for-profit educational or training institution which is to be found in many developed countries. In some types of adult provision, in countries such as France, the United States and the United Kingdom, the for-profit institution plays a major role (see Legave and Vignaud, 1979; Bendick, 1977; Williams and Woodhall, 1979). The second kind, upon which attention is focused here, is the publicly, privately or co-operatively owned enterprise whose training activities are subservient to its main business of producing and selling goods and services. The first kind of institution properly belongs to the for-profit sector. It is merely for convenience that it is here referred to as a for-profit educational institution, in recognition of the fact that education is its exclusive or primary business objective. The word enterprise is then reserved for that kind of for-profit enterprise — a firm or a single firm industry — where education is a subsidiary function.

Theoretical perspectives

An elegant neoclassical theory of the training behaviour of enterprises, so defined, has been developed over the last twenty years (see Becker, 1975). According to this theory the training undertaken by a firm can be classified as general, specific or a mixture of the two (see p. 28). The benefits from purely specific training are enjoyed solely by the firm, so it is willing to bear all the money and non-money costs of specific training. The profit-maximising firm calculates that it will recoup this investment from increased labour productivity over a period of years; and that the training will not increase the labour market value of the trainee because the skills are non-transferable. The effect of specificity on enterprise attitudes to financing training is also stressed by those labour market theorists who use an administrative model of enterprise behaviour which is quite different from Becker's model. 'The effect of skill specificity is two-fold: it encourages employers, rather than workers, to invest in training; once the investment has occurred it leads employers to stabilise employment and reduce turnover so that they can capture the benefits of training' (Doeringer and Piore, 1971). By contrast, general training imparts transferable skills, which the trained worker can take with her on leaving the firm and sell on the labour market for a skill premium in her earnings.

According to the theory, in a perfect market the risk of losing the return on its investment inhibits the firm from investing in general training. On the other hand, the trainee finds it worthwhile to finance her training by accepting wages below the value of her productivity while she is training. She finances general training because she can reap all the benefits, or sufficient to justify her costs, in the same way that the firm's certain enjoyment of the benefits from specific training leads it to finance that training. Sufficient trained workers to meet production requirements only come forward if the competition for skilled labour drives up skill differentials in wages to a level which gives a good return to the self-financing trainee. In a perfect market, if all skills are either purely general or purely specific, the entire cost of financing training would be precisely divided, according to the general/

specific nature of the training, between firms and workers. The incidence of financial cost tends to reflect the incidence of financial benefit. If training is specific in some ways and general in other respects, then the sharing of the cost burden between employer and employee will be proportionate to the ratio of specific to general training.

Becker's theory employs a number of heroic assumptions. For example, firms are omniscient profit-maximisers, buying labour and raising capital in perfectly competitive markets. That is to say, firms and workers buy and sell in markets with many completely-informed price-taking sellers and buyers. Goods and services of any kind are identical to each other and can be traded without any hindrances to free competition, e.g. no barriers to the entry of newcomers, no transport costs. In their accounts firms are able to separate out the costs of training from all other production costs. Their completely mobile and totally informed employees are intent on maximising the private return on any self-investment in skills. It is a positive theory. It tells us what will be the relationship between the nature of training and the distribution of the cost burden under specified conditions.

Testing this theory has proved to be extremely difficult. One reason is the frequent divergence between assumed and actual conditions under which enterprise training occurs. It is usually impossible to disentangle the effects of training investments by workers or by enterprises from the effects of the initial formal education of employees. The earnings differentials enjoyed by the most educated and highly trained workers over the less educated and trained are correlated simultaneously with length of initial education, length of work experience and possession of a range of personality traits which characterise trainability. Under modern conditions of team production, it is difficult to establish whether earnings differentials enjoyed by individuals really reflect the differential labour productivity of individuals. Indeed, there are sceptics who question the existence of straightforward and large effects from initial education or off-the-job training on productivity or earnings, and offer competing explanations of observed correlations between education and earnings differentials (e.g. Berg, 1971; Wiles, 1974; Fagerlind, 1975; Carnoy and Levin, 1976).

The actual behaviour of firms in relation to training frequently diverges from the behaviour to be expected of the profit-maximising firm in Becker's theory. One of the most obvious reasons for this divergence is the fact that, instead of a single-minded pursuit of profit, firms commonly have several objectives. Alternative hypotheses about their attitude to training could be derived from models of the non-profit-maximising firm (e.g. Cyert and March, 1963; Marris, 1964; Williamson, 1964). Firms may be trying to maximise sales revenue, their value on the stock market or the power and glory of their managers, subject to some constraint in terms of profitability such as a target rate of return on capital. In practice, many of the recruitment, remuneration, pension, training and industrial relations policies of firms are designed to reduce labour turnover by building loyalty and raising the cost of quitting the firm to the trained worker. Many other factors, in addition to company policy, conspire to inhibit geographical and occupational mobility. In consequence, it is safe for firms to finance some general training. Its cost can often be recouped.

Public policy on enterprise training

Becker's provocative theorising has driven economists to pay close attention to the relationship between labour turnover and the financing of training (e.g. Thomas, Moxham and Jones, 1969; Oatey, 1970; Makeham, 1978). In many European countries it is one of the goals of public policy to use education and training in order to improve the occupational and geographical mobility of labour. In this respect the United Kingdom probably lags behind some of its neighbours, partly because of attitudes in some firms and some unions. Employers tend to favour those ways of organising and financing training which will reduce labour turnover, and therefore labour mobility. Some unions in declining industries or occupations fear the consequences for their membership and revenues of enhancing the capacity of their members to move to new jobs or occupations, and to other unions.

In practice, adults with family responsibilities find it difficult to finance general training by accepting very low current earnings; and imperfections in the operation of balkanized labour markets, combined with housing difficulties, all reduce the mobility of labour. The lower the turnover, for whatever reason, the greater is the chance of a firm getting an adequate return on training in potentially transferable skills. In an imperfect non-Beckerian world, the greatest problem arises when firms become inhibited about financing general training, employees cannot afford to carry any large share of the costs themselves because they work in a low wage industry, and the overall level of training is judged to be sub-optimal.

In this situation, policymakers turn to compulsory schemes to spread
the costs of training between firms by earmarking part of their cash
flow. This happened in France with the law of July 16, 1971 and in the
United Kingdom with the 1964 Industrial Training Act. The analysis
underlying these legislative interventions is that some firms increase
the turnover of skilled labour by 'poaching' staff from firms which have
not yet received an adequate return on the cost of training them. All
firms become increasingly reluctant to finance training in transferable
skills; and the employee is in a weak financial position, compared with
his employer, to carry the burden herself. Whether or not this poaching hypothesis is sound is debateable (see Pettman, 1973; Ziderman,
1978; Drake, 1980). But the different French and British antidotes to
the industrial training problem, so defined, follow from the analysis.
By forcing firms to finance training up to certain levels they reduce the
incentive to 'poach', cut down on wastage and appear to increase the
corporate rate of return on training.

One of the notable characteristics of government interventions in
industrial training in countries like France and the United Kingdom is
that actual legislation, and alternatives which are proposed (e. g.
DE/MSC, 1976; Makeham, 1978), are firm-centred rather than worker-
centred. What are believed to be chronic shortages in transferable
skills are identified. Training remedies are proposed which reshuffle
between employers the costs of an increased volume of general training. There are bound to be some doubts, both about the accuracy of
the general analysis and about the presumed superiority of bureaucratic
estimation of skill requirements to estimation by users of skills. In a
country like the United Kingdom there are some indubitable skill
shortages, even in a time of severe unemployment. Some shortages
occur because of insufficient training. However, others occur for non-
training reasons, especially the under-utilisation or immobility of
skilled workers. These shortages may be more amenable to non-training
than to training remedies.

Very little systematic knowledge is available concerning substitution
between different kinds of skilled labour, and between more and less
skilled labour. However, 'bad' training decisions may not result in
serious consequences if different kinds of labour can be substituted for
each other. To some extent, the notion of underfinancing of training by
firms depends on the assumption that there is a fixed relationship
between any given level of production and a 'requirement' of skills,
without which that level is unattainable. In certain cases, it is clear

that a precisely defined level of skill and number of working hours is
essential if a job is to be safely and effectively completed. But there is
little evidence that the relationship between output and skilled labour is
generally fixed. Some of the most thorough studies suggest that, in
many occupations and industries, the productivity or profit penalties for
substituting less for more skilled labour can be negligible and are rarely
large or certain (see Layard et al, 1971; Dougherty, 1972). Technically,
there is much scope for flexible use of skills, provided that the financing decisions of firms are not constrained by bureaucratically-
determined training norms. It is not clear that there exists an adequate
knowledge base for some of the more ambitious public policies on
industrial training; or that these policies represent an efficient solution
to the problems which arise when training decisions are left entirely to
firms and, by implication, workers.

Enterprise financing in practice

In practice, firms often behave in a non-Beckerian way (e. g. Thomas,
Moxham and Jones, 1969; Ryan, 1980). Many firms train people in
transferable skills either because labour turnover is low enough to
enable them to recoup training costs through higher productivity, or
because they consider that 'being a good trainer' and paying trainees
more than is necessary to attract good applicants are sensible constraints on the pursuit of other company objectives. As the manager of
one American shipyard company welding school put it, not without pride:
'we're training for the whole region' (Ryan, 1980, p.344).

New technologies have always been essentially regenerative, destroying
old jobs but creating new ones in order to supply new products and new
services. One recent US Secretary of Labor pointed out that if American
banks were to provide the same services as they do now, without any of
the office technology installed since World War Two, they would need to
employ every adult woman in the United States (quoted by Merritt, 1982,
p. 22). In practice, the rate of introduction of labour-saving technologies
is not determined by mere availability, nor by a ruthless and single-
minded corporate pursuit of profit. The degree of competition in an
industry, labour market conditions, and the local industrial relations
climate and customs are major factors. So a large British insurance
company continued to train 900 fresh recruits a year for clerical grades
at the end of the seventies, though the office technology was available
off the shelf to cut its clerical workforce from 4,500 to 1,500.

(i)   Determinants of training behaviour

The training decisions of British firms may be best understood in
terms of an almost Beckerian investment appraisal modified —
sometimes out of all recognition — by variables such as

- the firm's self-image;

- its experience of the search and recruitment costs involved in
  'poaching' skilled workers;

- the levy-grant-exemption scheme of an Industry Training Board;

- considerations of occupational status;

- the place of training in collective bargaining;

- the economic state of the particular firm and industry;

- the degree of labour mobility;

- elasticities of substitution between different skill levels and
  between capital and labour;

- and present and anticipated rates of unemployment locally,
  regionally and nationally.

The total volume of training financed by firms is bound to be influenced
heavily by the level of economic activity and by company expectations
about the future. However, even with the British economy in deep
recession in 1982, there were probably about seven million job changes
in the year and between a half and three quarters of a million new
entrants to the labour force. Nine out of ten job vacancies in Britain
are for skilled jobs. Aside from technological change, this ebb and flow
creates a perpetual necessity for induction training and for more
advanced varieties which employers can generally be relied upon to
finance, jointly with those initial trainees whose training wages are lower
than the value of their output. In 1976/77 the British economy was not
in a notably healthy condition. But a recent estimate suggests that
between three and four million workers aged 19 and above received some
form of educational leave paid for by their employers during that year.
This is about one in six of the workforce. It represents between 25 and
30 million training days, some 8 days per trainee, or an annual rate of
approximately $1\frac{1}{2}$ days per head of the entire workforce. Over two
million of these trainees attended courses which were provided and
probably financed in-house, and many of the remaining million or more
were on courses financed entirely by employers (Killeen and Bird, 1981).

In many European countries firms have for long relied on tax-financed post-secondary educational institutions to provide large infusions of young people with technician or degree level qualifications, industry's qualified and highly qualified manpower. In the case of lower level technicians and skilled manpower, firms have generally carried a larger share of the financing burden themselves, but increasingly in conjunction with tax-financed vocational schools or technical colleges. This trend towards additional tax-financing is to be found even in high apprenticeship countries like West Germany (see Winterhager, 1980). The training of these youngest adults, especially at the skilled and lower technician levels, has tended to suffer in some countries as a result of cyclical change — recession and unemployment hitting the younger workers with disproportionate force — but also as a result of structural change. In the United Kingdom, for example, manufacturing employment fell from 8.1 million workers in 1968 to 6.7 million in 1980. But the number of initial training places fell 36 per cent while employment dropped by 17 per cent. While this employment-based initial training financed by firms was contracting, education-based initial training financed out of taxation expanded.

In recent years European governments have had to watch an erosion of training opportunities or provide more and more tax support as firms drew back. Many countries have compelled firms to contribute at least a minimum proportion of their cash flow to training (see ILO, 1979). Sweden and Denmark have adopted forms of payroll tax. Under legislation of 1971, 1976 and 1978 French firms with more than 10 employees were by 1978 contributing 1.1 per cent of their total wage bill to financing continuing training in one or more of five modes:

- by subscribing to an employers' training organisation;
- by contributing to a training insurance fund (FAF);
- by training their own workers;
- by paying up to 10 per cent of the compulsory contributions to approved organisations;
- by paying the compulsory contributions to the public treasury.

In particular, this legislation aimed to increase labour mobility as well as helping the disadvantaged and assuring a minimum level of enterprise financing (Legave and Vignaud, 1979; Vincent, 1980). Despite such measures, several countries have not been able to maintain the previous volume and quality of initial training opportunities for adults.

Firms continue to invest three to four per cent of total personnel costs in initial and continuing training in the United Kingdom, as in other Western European countries (Johnson, 1979; Woodhall, 1980; Edding, 1981). But this is not always enough to provide sufficient training opportunities for very large numbers of young adults, and retraining for the victims of structural economic change and of recession, on top of the requirement to upgrade work force skills in the face of technological change and world-wide competition.

(ii) <u>Strengths and weaknesses of enterprise practice</u>

In the United Kingdom nearly 60 per cent of all trainees in manufacturing are employed in establishments of 250 or more employees, at which plant size firms are often able not only to finance but to provide a range of specialised training opportunities in-house. Big multinationals, like Shell, Unilever, IBM or Philips, each have an annual turnover which exceeds in value the gross domestic product of a country like Eire or Portugal. This cash flow gives them a formidable capacity to finance their own training requirements. For instance, in 1981 Unilever claimed world-wide sales worth almost £12 billion, of which £8 billion was in European countries and £1½ billion in North America. It employed 343,000 workers in the 75 countries in which it operated, 170,000 of these in Europe and 21,000 in North America. Consider only one group of employees: managers. They require expensive initial and continuing training. There were 20,000 in the company in 1981 (Unilever, 1982). The Nestle Group can be used to illustrate a multinational's training operation in one country (see Table 6, page 86). The 1981 annual report of the Nestle Company Ltd showed that it had 7,633 full-time UK employees. No fewer than 5,147 participated in some kind of training or education during the year, averaging six training days per participant. In addition, 59 craft apprentices and 51 other full-time trainees were employed during the year. Like many 'good trainers' the company seriously understates its training costs. The total declared cost of training excludes the considerable wage and salary costs of persons being trained off the job, although it includes company training centre expenditures and all other costs. Even this undercosting of £650,000 amounts to £126 per participant. Many large and medium-sized companies continue to train heavily in stagnating economies, the major exceptions being in those manufacturing industries which are in steep decline.

Table 6:   Nestle UK Company Training

	Participants	Training Days
Planned on-the-job training within the company	1,536	14,253
Off-the-job training within the company	2,731	5,585
Training within the Group abroad	18	171
Training with outside organisations	739	6,811
Day release courses	123	4,318
	5,147	31,138

Source: 1981 Annual Report, Nestle Company Ltd

The financing role of firms is influenced by the size of the firm and by the branch of the economy. For example, in France in 1978, the actual rate of financial participation by employers ranged from 0.85 per cent of payroll for small enterprises to 2.9 per cent for those employing a staff of more than 2,000; and from 0.93 per cent in the hotel and restaurant trade to 4.41 per cent in the production and distribution of electricity, gas and water (Legave and Vignaud, 1979, p.77). The obligatory participation for French employers is 1.1 per cent of payroll, but 0.2 per cent is devoted to measures to combat youth unemployment and unemployment among women of all ages. So the employer may allocate 0.9 per cent to continuing training of his choice. However, actual enterprise spending on training far exceeds this minimum. In 1980 almost 1.7 million employees in about 120,000 enterprises benefited from training courses on which firms spent FF10 milliard (1976: FF 6.5 milliard). The actual financial contribution by firms was almost double the legal minimum: 1.6 per cent against 0.9 per cent of payroll (Le Figaro, 10.9.82, p.12).

Even in a country with a very strong tradition of financing of training
by small as well as large firms, such as West Germany, this financing
is sensitive in aggregate to cyclical as well as structural change; and
sensitive in its distribution to considerations of individual productivity
(see Winterhager, 1980). In consequence, enterprises underfinance
certain groups among employed adults. These are workers who are not
always inherently less trainable than others, but from whom the yield
of increased productivity is less certain. One of the largest of these
disadvantaged groups is women workers. In 1980, out of an employed
UK labour force of 24.7 million, 58 per cent were men and 42 per cent
women. But two-fifths of the women were part-time compared with one-
twentieth of the men. In the United Kingdom women have notably higher
absenteeism and turnover rates than men. There is legislation which
prohibits even full-time women workers from working over a certain
number of hours per week or at certain times. These characteristics
are regarded as one of the main reasons why employers have less
incentive to pay for female than for male training: it is more difficult
for an employer to get a satisfactory return on training costs (Metcalf
and Richardson, 1980, p.272).

The same phenomena are sometimes held responsible for the reluctance
of girls and women, compared with men, to invest in themselves. But
it is impossible to decide to what extent the under-training of the female
labour force reflects a rational employer calculation of costs weighed
against a discounted, interrupted and uncertain benefit stream; and to
what extent it simply reflects a female demand for training frustrated
by an occupational and training structure profoundly biased against
women. The British initial education system is slightly less biased than
the post-initial, but even so it has produced a stock of highly qualified
males who outnumber highly qualified females 3 to 1. Unregulated
financing by firms does tend to lead to some failures on grounds of
efficiency or equity. Training investments which are too risky for
individual firms may be more easily financed by spreading the risk between likely users of skills, and using some form of collective funding
between firms, with or without an admixture of tax funds (see Department of Employment, 1976). In countries like France and the United
Kingdom provision of training to aid occupational and geographical
mobility, to assist the introduction of new technologies, or to counteract
corporate under-investment among the groups of disadvantaged employees have all been grounds for government interventions and the use of
tax funds.

When firms finance a particular kind of training collectively they are often dealing with a free rider problem, and financing training collectively to a level in excess of that which they would finance individually. They are then financing a collective-type good for a subset of all employers, where the benefits of training are not confined to one employer but spill over to all users. When governments add in some tax funds, or finance training entirely out of tax funds, they seek to compensate for the biases or the inadequacies of enterprise financing. In some cases, benefits spill over widely among employers and others, for example benefits from the existence of retraining capacity to enhance occupational and geographical mobility. In other cases, the benefits from public financing are captured by a few firms, for example those using new technologies, or by groups of individuals, such as the disadvantaged employees.

(iii) Government interventions

Many of the disagreements about enterprise training focus on the extent and object of government interventions in its financing. Certainly, firms make errors of judgement in assessing their likely manpower requirements. Or they take a short-term view, at the expense of their long-term health and that of the economy. In either eventuality, underfinancing of training may occur. In the first case, underfinancing is probably a more likely consequence than overfinancing; in the second case, it might be held to occur by definition, provided that there is a long run. The alternative to such underfinancing is to award the power to allocate enterprise funds to legislatures, which set minimum spending levels; or to the bureaucratic discretion of 'representative' committees, to civil servants or to 'experts'. These are all people who tend to sit well back from the production of goods and services, and are not required to live too intimately with the consequences of their allocative decisions. It is a moot point whose mistakes are going to be the more serious, those of the enterprises or of their surrogates.

In recent years West European governments have tended, in varying degrees, to concentrate the use of tax funds on enhancing the mobility of workforces, while pursuing social equity among the employed and employability and trainability for jobseekers. Beyond the initial education system, the task of financing training for higher productivity is generally left in the hands of employers, with limited public intervention as to minimum levels of spending in countries like France, Denmark and, partially, the United Kingdom. In these countries, the setting of training objectives is no longer left entirely in the hands of employers, even when training is being financed exclusively by them. But corporate training objectives remain preponderant. In the United Kingdom there has even been a re-assertion of the primacy of the goals of the individual firm, signalled by the rejection of the 1976 proposals for collective funding and the 1982 dismantling of sixteen ITBs in favour of voluntary arrangements between firms. But it is difficult to believe that, in the long run, public legislative, regulatory and financial interventions will not be used increasingly to complement and to influence the level and distribution of training finance by firms. Such interventions will serve public goals like full employment, the easing of structural change in economies, and the provision of better training opportunities for women, the handicapped, immigrants and those discriminated against on grounds of age — in general, the youngest and oldest members of the labour force.

It is easier for governments to intervene in order to influence the level and distribution of training finance than it is to intervene more profoundly, for example in the distribution of specific skills which are learned on the job. Learning by experience has sometimes been classified as training (e.g. Mincer, 1962; Thomas, Moxham and Jones, 1969) but is here called learning by experience. Skills which are acquired through trial and error can often be acquired more quickly, and at greater explicit cost, with the help of an experienced worker or instructor. Then the essential choice is between learning by experience on the job and without formal training, and learning on the job with training, if one ignores the intermediate process of task and job rotation deliberately contrived as a learning programme (see Oatey, 1970, pp. 3-5).

On the job training which is more than learning by experience can be regarded as an application of additional resources to accelerate and to guide learning which might have occurred by trial and error, and would have involved no one besides the learning adult. It is is not easy to determine the optimal combination of on the job learning with and without training. But some national training policies influence the selection by firms of combinations of these two forms of learning with each other and with off the job training. It is sometimes assumed that the policy-induced combinations are improvements, a closer approximation to some optimum mix of learning modes.

In the United Kingdom, the 1964 Industrial Training Act and the 1973 Employment and Training Act produced policies, and financial interventions by ITBs and the MSC, which appear to have shifted existing combinations by favouring off the job training and to a lesser degree, on

the job learning with training. However, systematic evidence on the
actual combinations used by firms is very difficult to find. The gains
and losses of each mode, which should guide the choice of modes, are
a matter of some dispute. Oatey (1970, p. 6) has argued that on-the-
job learning without training can be very costly to the firm up to a
criterion level of skill, but is thereafter costless. This is debatable.
However, the argument is that learning by experience without training
can continue after performance has reached the criterion level. If
learning by experience has no opportunity cost to the firm, then the
firm has to look very carefully at any proposal for training on or off-
the-job which is designed to improve performance above the criterion
level. Such training will have financial costs, and the performance
improvement attributable to those costs is not the total improvement
but the difference between the cost-less improvement from further
learning by experience and the costly improvement recorded after
training.

The consequences of government financial interventions for the choice
of learning modes, though important, remain obscure. In addition to
influencing the distribution of skills indirectly through interventions
in off-the-job and on-the-job training, governments have also taken
limited steps directly to influence the distribution of those skills which
are learned on the job. Most of these tentative interventions take the
form of full or partial funding of workplace opportunities for young
adults between sixteen and twenty years old. Such programmes are too
recent, and too sensitive politically, to have been properly evaluated
for their long-term effects on the distribution of skills or even for their
effects on in-firm productivity. However, this kind of intervention in
the use of labour by firms does take government intervention to the heart
of enterprise training. The fundamental feature of such training is not
off-the-job training inside or outside the firm. Off-the-job training is
the kind of training which is most frequently costed and evaluated. But,
in general, on-the-job learning, by experience or with training, is
quantitatively a more important mode of learning. Moreover, employer-
financed off-the-job training only occurs after a firm has decided to
employ a person and allocate her to a particular job. Except for manual
labour and other totally unskilled work, employment means access to
some kind of employer-financed training. For those in the primary
labour market, it means access to a series of jobs and to a training
ladder. An offer of a job is an offer of employer-financed training
ranging from half-a-day's induction to a long series of expensive in-
house and off-the-job training programmes. In this aspect, employment

policy is properly regarded as an arm of public policy on training opportunities. In many cases, an opportunity to earn is an opportunity to learn. Hiring and firing open and close learning opportunities.

It may be that skills acquired on the job are even more unequally distributed than skills acquired in formal education. Thurow (1982) argues that skills acquired on the job are the standard explanation for variance in earnings between individual members of any group with a homogeneous profile of formal education. But the relationship between skills acquired during formal education and skills acquired on the job is not easy to establish and is under-researched. At best, the screening hypothesis, which ties hirings to educational qualifications in a tight and hierarchical way, relates only to first jobs. After that, many employees in developed countries find themselves in internal labour markets where job performance counts for more than formal educational qualifications, both for promotion and for access to further training.

Are skills acquired on-the-job and skills acquired off-the-job complements or substitutes? In which circumstances, and in which occupations? When they are complements, the firm has a powerful incentive to hire people with appropriate educational qualifications, or to finance employees to acquire them, because the productivity of their on-the-job learning depends on complementary skills from off-the-job training. When they are substitutes, the firm is bound to look at the cost of financing their acquisition off-the-job compared with the cost to the firm of their acquisition on-the-job. Those who believe that on-the-job learning is costless once a criterion skill level is attained appear to be thinking in terms of cash transactions implied by training. One of the prime justifications for carefully structured on-the-job training is a reduction of output losses as a result of accelerated learning. What happens after the criterion level is reached? While learning continues, there must still be output losses up to the point where output per person is maximised. The only question is whether resource commitments to raise skills above a criterion level are worthwhile when set against costs measured in terms of the output losses, wastages of material and wear and tear which constitute for most firms the main cost of on-the-job learning.

If it is true that skills acquired on the job dominate the distribution of all skills and the distribution of earnings (see Thurow, 1982, p. 76), the significance of this for public policy is considerable. It is unlikely that the distribution of on-the-job training and, more fundamentally, the distribution of on-the-job learning, can be determined by public budgets or by legislative interventions. This distribution is central to the management function in enterprises. Under prevailing political conditions in developed countries, it is effectively outside the range of government interventions in the public as well as the private sector of their economies. The most attainable goals for these governments are a dominant influence in the distribution of skills acquired during initial formal education, and a lesser influence on the distribution of skills acquired during off-the-job training.

HOUSEHOLDS

In the adult education industry households occupy a unique position. They are at the same time one of the original sources of funds for education and training (see Figures 2 and 3, pages 21-22), and the basic unit of social organisation, to which all adult learners belong. Alongside enterprises, it is households which provide all the funds for the public sector, except those which are borrowed from the banking system. Households also provide funds to parafiscs through subscriptions and donations. A large proportion of the funds allocated by government or parafiscs have first been transferred compulsorily or voluntarily from households. In addition to this wholesale transfer of funds to two other sectors of the industry, households spend directly on educational services by paying fees to or purchasing educational materials from publicly-maintained, parafiscal and for-profit institutions. Adult members of the household are also citizens, members of parafiscal organisations and employees. From time to time membership of one body or the other may lapse, for example if they become unemployed or retire from paid work. But the most typical learner is a multi-role adult. In one or more of these roles he is frequently learning, and this learning is often structured and partially resourced by others.

A unit of resource and of finance

In some kinds of adult learning the household itself is the dominant unit of resource and the dominant unit of finance. It is necessary to distinguish between the overlapping functions of the household as a unit of resource and as a unit of finance. As a unit of resource the household commands a range of marketable and unmarketable capital assets, and an income which can also be used in support of the learning activities of its adult members. Some assets are physical capital such as houses, television sets, books, microcomputers and motor cars. Some are more liquid financial assets, i. e. assets which can easily be turned into money, such as savings deposits. Some are unmarketable financial assets like occupational pension rights or the right to a variety of transfer payments from the state in virtue of a status such as the single parent in a one parent family, or being unemployed or retired. The household has at its disposal human capital in the skills, knowledge and values of its members; and adults have at their disposal whatever time is not contracted to someone else by engaging in paid work. As a unit of resource the household can deploy physical assets, human capital and the time of its members in aid of learning. As a unit of finance it can commit to educational purposes part of its money income and any of its marketable wealth that it is prepared to turn into income.

For many analytical purposes it is probably safe to simplify this complex economic organisation by saying that each household has a stock of physical and human capital, a disposable time budget and a disposable money budget. When the deployment of its capital and disposable time is being considered, the household is viewed as a collection of resources. When the disposal of its money income is in question, the household is viewed as a financing unit. The unit of finance is a subset of the unit of resource. Some resources which are not included in the unit of finance can nevertheless be converted into money (liquid financial assets) or substituted for money (disposable time). So the subset frontier between the unit of finance and the unit of resource is, in effect, permeable. Disposable income represents one part of the household's total command over resources. It is normally deployed by simultaneously drawing on non-money resources such as the time budget of individual members or the household's stock of physical and human capital.

In other kinds of learning, for example job-related learning or learning which follows from membership of a voluntary non-profit organisation, a larger proportion of resources and of funds comes from outside the household itself. But resourcing and financing is still a partnership. Forms of adult education where the household does not make at least a small financial contribution, e. g. in the form of travel expenses or purchase of books and materials, are quite rare. Even rarer are adult learning activities where there is no resource cost at all to the household. Any individual who has an alternative use for her scarce time incurs a private cost by devoting that time to learning. By accepting wages below the value of her output during training an adult reduces present for future income.

Perspectives on household behaviour

For these reasons the level of resources and money income available to households, and constraints upon the use of resources and income, should be a central concern in the economics and finance of adult education. The household is coming to be regarded by economists as a micro-economy. It has to keep under rolling review the allocation of assets, money income and time between competing uses, for instance between paid work, unpaid work and leisure (see Shultz, 1974; Ghez and Becker, 1975; Eide, 1981). One of the most trenchant but constructive critics of the new (Chicago) theory of the household assesses it thus :

> 'Traditional theory views the family as a one-person household, maximising a utility function that is defined on goods and services bought in the marketplace. The new economics of the family instead views the family as a multiperson production unit, maximising a production function whose inputs are market goods and the time, skills and knowledge of different members of the family. The result is not only to extend the standard tools of microeconomics to problems usually assigned to the domain of sociology, social psychology and social anthropology but to transform the traditional explanation of consumer behaviour. ' (Blaug, 1980, p. 240).

Traditionally, economists have relied almost exclusively on price and income variations to explain the decisions of single-person households. The emerging research programme shuns ad hoc explanations of household behaviour in terms of changing tastes. Instead, it adds to the traditional explanatory variables of income and price a widening range of socio-economic conditions, e. g. occupation, initial education, race, household size and age structure. Such a research programme may have considerable potential for explaining the decisions of households in resourcing and in financing the education of adult members. Governments, employers and parafiscs have until now appeared as the chief actors in adult education. But an enriched understanding of the major but neglected role of the household may be attainable. Instead of viewing educational decisions as a function of an individual's money income and of the money price which he faces, decisions can be seen as a function of a complex endowment of which money income is merely one part. Educational decisions can be seen as a response not just to a money price, but to a set of constraints and opportunities, including a time price.

The household choice set, within which the decision about learning is to be taken, does not exist merely at one moment in time. It is extended forward over time by the perceptions of the choosers, by imaginative projection. Moreover, the individual belongs during his life to a succession of households, each of which will profoundly and in different ways influence his behaviour. The individual may begin as a junior member of a family, but he graduates to be a single, independent grown-up, a new one-person household. He may then merge with another one-person household to establish a new household, including children and adults, which survives for twenty or thirty years; after which the household diminishes again as children leave and founding adults die (see Drake and Rasmussen, 1981, pp. 13-22). The household invests time, other resources and disposable income especially in its children and younger adult members. Much of this heavy investment is not accounted and recognised in the same way as the complementary public investment in the initial education of the young or even the poorly-documented employer investment in off-the-job and on-the-job training.

Inequalities between households

(i) Virtuous and vicious multipliers

Household, public and corporate investments in the individual vary widely; and, in particular, according to household income, social class and culture as a proxy for household values, and according to the race, sex, age, ability and occupation of the learner. These variations are systematic. There are strong inter-correlations between household, public and corporate investments in the individual. In developed countries, a disproportionate share of public and corporate investment tends to be added to prolonged and heavy household investment in the individual. This is the well-known fortunate multiplier: to those that have, more is given. One aspect of this phenomenon is clear from data on public educational spending in Britain, and from the 1980 Family Expenditure Survey. The Central Statistical Office's analysis of the effects of taxes and benefits on household income has to be treated with great caution because only 58 per cent of government revenue and 46 per cent of expenditure in 1980 could be allocated to households.

Nevertheless, the distribution of public educational spending by household income in Table 7 is almost certainly correct in showing that the
higher its income the more public educational spending a household
enjoys. Indeed, the data may understate the inequality.

Table 7: Average value of educational benefits assigned to each
household ranked by original income 1980

Quintile group	£ per household
Bottom fifth	190
Next fifth	310
Middle fifth	510
Next fifth	600
Top fifth	630
Average all households	450

Source: Table G in 'The effects of taxes and benefits on household
income 1980', Economic Trends, January 1982.

There is often very much less public or corporate spending on training
or retraining of individuals of any age from the least advantaged households. From those households come many of the young adults with the
poorest learning bases.

(ii) The limitations of public intervention

As the young emerge into adulthood they do so with a fortunate or
unfortunate inheritance, with an advantageous or a disadvantageous
history of household investment in their education and training. They
establish new households; but not from scratch. Some new households
are the beneficiaries of the virtuous investment multiplier, while others
are handicapped from the beginning by the vicious multiplier of household under-investment in education. Adult education may reinforce or
counteract these virtuous and vicious multipliers operating throughout
people's lives. But it is difficult to break cycles of advantage or of

deprivation once people have reached adulthood. One very direct method of reviving household economies devastated by unemployment is to tackle hard-core adult unemployment with a mixture of training and jobs. Cash benefits for the unemployed account for at least one-third of the fiscal cost of unemployment even in a low-productivity, low wage and low benefit economy like Britain's. When central government looks at this growing bill it is bound to consider schemes to fund jobs (in which people can produce and learn) and training (in which people learn). But spending public money to help them and their households can easily suffer from diminishing returns as unemployment deepens. In the United Kingdom, the Manpower Services Commission has had to admit the declining cost-effectiveness of spending on its major programme of speculative off-the-job training for adults, the Training Opportunities Scheme. As labour market conditions have worsened, placement rates have dropped to about 35 per cent, the worst placement rates being those from expensive government-owned Skillcentres specialising in those older craft skills which are under such pressure from technical change and from structural shifts in the British economy (MSC, 1982, p.10).

To make significant changes to the fundamental processes by which social class so frequently governs, or at least influences, access to learning opportunities is extremely difficult in a country like the United Kingdom. Since World War Two, there have been repeated efforts to reform the initial education system so that adults will be less constrained by the endowment of the household in which they grew up. But attempts to produce greater equality of access to learning opportunities for all social classes have largely failed (see Goldthorpe et al, 1980; Halsey et al, 1980). Many would agree with Le Grand's conclusion :

'The provision of free education has created neither equality of use, cost, public expenditure or outcome. Indeed, it is possible in some cases it may actually have promoted greater inequality. The reason for this appears to be the pervasive influence of the structure of broader social and economic inequality, a structure that itself seems largely impervious to educational reform' (Le Grand, 1982, p. 79).

Even in Sweden, a sustained effort over many decades has not been notably successful. Fagerlind researched the role of formal education as an institutional link between social background factors and the subsequent occupational status and earnings of adults. Longitudinal data on people from childhood to the age of 43 (in 1971) was used: 1,544 children who were aged 10 in 1938 in Malmo, Sweden.

The entire range of ability and income was covered. Educational attainment was measured by IQ tests at 10 and 20 and by length and level of schooling; income data came from public records, social data by interview and questionnaire. In 1971 information was available for 90 per cent of respondents, and for any one variable it exceeded 70 per cent. Fagerlind (1975, p. 78) concluded that, in Sweden, a person's destiny is set by the first household of which he is a member. The amount and consequences of adult learning depends on whether he is caught in a virtuous or a vicious multiplier:

> 'The resources the individual has access to in early childhood, mainly family resources and personality assets, are converted into "marketable" assets mainly through the formal education system... Later assets, such as the quality of the education, have both strong direct and indirect effects on earnings. The school system alone is not an adequate instrument for equalising opportunities. This is because educational benefits are best used by those who come from an advantaged background. Without some kind of equalisation of home and childhood resources the educational system will function as a stratifier, wherein successful performances in one socialised setting are used to justify different and more advantageous treatments in the next. The resource conversions which take place in the home, in the school and on the job act in such a way as to decrease equality over the life cycle instead of increasing it.'

British household inequalities: nature and size

Adults inherit values as well as property and contacts. Potentially the most important resource, in countering the inequalities of their genetic, social and economic inheritance, is the household in which they live as adults. These households are unequal. In a number of developed countries their number has risen and their size diminished in recent decades. In 1981 the United Kingdom had a total population of 55.9 million, of which 34.7 million were aged 16-64 years and another 8.2 million were 65 years old and older. Of these 43 million adults (aged 16 and over), some 24.7 million were employed or self-employed in 1980. The number of households has been increasing in the United Kingdom, from 16.6 million in 1960 to 18.9 million in 1971 and 20.9 million in 1979, by which year there were on average 2.7 persons per household, 23 per cent of the total being single person households.

These British data suggest that the financial capacity of households may have been eroded in recent decades simply because of their proliferation, though the consequences of this for the financing of adult learning has not been investigated. A similar phenomenon is to be seen in the United States, where the number of single parent families rose from 12.1 per cent of all families with children in 1970 to 19.1 per cent in 1980, and the number of people living alone rose dramatically to 18 million by 1980. In the United States the median household income of $16,830 a year in 1979 bought no more than the median household income in 1969. But real income per capita had grown during that period by over 18 per cent, to $7,313. Medians and means are crude measures and difficult to compare, but this divergence of median household and mean per capita incomes does provide a very rough indicator of the way in which changes in number and size can damage the financing capacity of the household.

There are two forms of inequality in household spending on education. Primary inequality is caused by the serious lack of wealth and income in some households. Then the household's capacity to finance learning is crippled. Secondary inequality occurs because income is only trans- muted into educational spending through the intervention of certain values. Many households enjoy quite good levels of wealth and income, but few resources and little money are devoted to learning because the prevailing attitude is one of indifference or even hostility to education. Education often seeks to and sometimes succeeds in changing values, so educational remedies are appropriate to the reduction of secondary inequality between households. By contrast, primary inequality is a straightforward problem of the distribution of wealth and income.

The size of the total problem of resource and financial inequality between households can be gauged from United Kingdom data. Although the distribution of wealth in Britain is far more equal today than it was at the beginning of the century, there are still very large inequalities between households. These inequalities are largest in the ownership of marketable wealth. In 1979, according to the Inland Revenue, the wealthiest one per cent of the population aged 18 years and over, owned 24 per cent of all marketable wealth and the top 10 per cent owned 59 per cent. Just 41 per cent of marketable wealth was left for the remain- ing 90 per cent of the population (Social Trends No. 12, 1981, Table 5.26). However, the top one per cent, who own 24 per cent of marketable wealth, are usually estimated to account for only 5 to 6 per cent of all before tax incomes (see Diamond Commission, 1979). In 1978-79 the income difference between the top and bottom 10 per cent of incomes was reduced from over ten to one before tax to eight to one after tax, and after tax incomes are probably more appropriate than pre-tax incomes to a consideration of the autonomous financing capacity of households (Social Trends No. 12, 1981, Table 5.23). In 1978-79, the top 10 per cent of persons, who enjoyed 23.4 per cent of all after tax income, clearly had a financial capacity far superior to persons in the lower deciles of the distribution. The bottom 10 per cent had only 2.9 per cent of all after tax income and the next four deciles (81-90, 71-80, 61-70, 51-60 per cent) had respectively 4.1, 5.1, 6.4 and 7.7 per cent. So the after tax income of the top tenth was at least three times as great as that enjoyed by any of the five bottom tenths. (Social Trends No. 12, 1981, Table 5.23)

Marketable wealth is an important component in the financing capacity of a household. But even non-marketable wealth, like pension rights, is bound to affect the willingness and capacity of households to engage in the financing of educational activities. There are three kinds of household income: investment income, employment income and transfer income. Investment income comes from the ownership of property. Of the three kinds of income, it is the most unevenly distributed. It is also quantitatively less important than employment or transfer incomes, except to a minute number of extremely wealthy households. The distribution of all household incomes is dominated by the two main components of household incomes. Income from employment and self-employment accounted for 73 per cent of total household incomes in 1980, grants from public authorities (transfer incomes) another 13 per cent, and only 14 per cent from all other income sources, including investment income and private pensions (Social Trends No. 12, 1981, Table 5.1). The distribution of household incomes is less unequal than the distribution of all wealth, which is in turn less unequal than the distribution of marketable wealth.

Income inequalities between households are not as severe as they are between individuals. It may be that, for most purposes concerned with learning, the real unit of decision-making, resourcing and financing is the household rather than the individual adult or even the family — though the extended family can still be an important resource in some developed countries. At the root of household income inequalities is the inequality of employment incomes, which can in turn be traced to a number of inter-correlated causes, notably to differences between adult members in age, work experience, hours worked, race, sex and family

background. Put another way, the observed distribution of earnings
between individuals reflects a complex interaction between the underlying distribution of values, abilities and opportunities. One of the
most important causes of earning inequalities is the coupling of natural
ability with education and training. In the United Kingdom the unequal
distribution of natural ability between individuals is aggravated by a
tendency among those who are working class, non-white or female not
to have their natural ability fully developed by either initial or continuing education. One of the factors depressing the capacity of certain
households to finance education and training is the lack of education and
training, and consequent low earnings, of their adult members. On
average, education is positively associated with earnings. The key
relationships have been summarised thus :

'If, for a given level of formal training, a man comes to the labour
market with relatively great motivation, ability and drive he will
tend to earn more than the average worker. Further, it is estab-
lished that on average the more naturally gifted man tends to undertake more than average amounts of training. An unskewed distribution of ability combined with a skewed distribution of training
produces a skewed distribution of productivity. The last, in an
approximately competitive market, produces a skewed earnings
distribution' (Metcalf and Richardson, 1980, p.263).

Low pay, as well as unemployment, causes serious primary inequality
between households. Some two million adults in the United Kingdom are
functionally illiterate, and it is particularly difficult for them to get
anything other than a very badly paid job. By 1981 unskilled manual
workers were earning less in relation to average earnings than in 1886.
Some 3 million adults impoverished by unemployment were matched by
nearly 5 million more adults who were employed full-time in lower paid
jobs and another 2 to 3 million adults in very poorly paid part-time work.
In 1981 roughly two-fifths of the labour force were earning at or below
a £75 per week breadline (Merritt, 1982, pp.80-81).

Government may help to reduce employment income inequalities, either
by across-the-board equality, as in state pension schemes, or by concentrating transfer payments on the most needy households. In the
United Kingdom social security payments of all kinds total almost one
quarter of all government spending. When these transfer incomes are
added to investment and employment incomes they further reduce
financial inequalities between households. But one in ten of the British

population still lives in a family which depends on transfer payments to achieve even a poverty-level income (see Townsend, 1979).

Of course, households are interested in learning opportunities beyond those which will help them out of the economic pit. Households whose adult members suffer from unemployment or low pay are bound to look towards training, for jobs or for better wages, despite their extremely limited capacity to resource such learning themselves. But large groups of disadvantaged adults have additional objectives. Immigrants in Brixton (London), Kreuzberg (West Berlin) or Vitry-sur-Seine (Paris) require not merely an economic lifebelt but a road towards socialisation and acceptance. The huge and growing populations of those who have retired from paid work are searching for fresh horizons and new friendships.

In 1982 a counsellor to the President of the United States was reported to have declared that 'the progressive income tax is immoral' (Economist, 26.6.82, p.35). He was not alone in that sentiment. There is always an important degree of resistance to the notion of taxing household incomes in order to finance spending on behalf of adults, instead of leaving a larger proportion of household income to be allocated and spent by the household themselves. There is always a degree of resistance to a redistribution of purchasing power from richer to poorer households. Even those who accept existing levels of taxation of household incomes may not approve a further reduction in the financial autonomy of households.

Some would argue from past data, that an expansion of public or corporate spending is unnecessary because household spending on learning will expand if real incomes increase. Even between 1975 and 1980 real disposable household income per head in Britain seems to have risen by 15 per cent (Social Trends No. 12, 1981, Table 5.1). Recent history suggests that educational spending tends to increase at least in step with disposable household incomes. Disposable time is increasing, and it is arguable that time is getting cheaper, as the amount of paid work time shrinks and time for unpaid work and leisure increases. Some would argue that any further allocation of resources to learning, at the expense of other household activities, should be left to households to decide. On the other hand, even if average household income and average personal spending on learning rose in the eighties, it seems highly likely that the disparaties in household incomes would continue to produce very serious inequalities in their capacity to finance learning.

CHAPTER FIVE : MARKETS AND BUREAUCRACIES

There is a broad but useful distinction between market and bureaucratic allocation of resources to education. Under a regime of market alloca- tion, financial instruments such as fees and subscriptions produce a large proportion of all funds used to finance the activity. A defining characteristic of these financial instruments is that they relate the amount which is paid to the use of instructional services. Under a regime of bureaucratic or administrative allocation, this direct link between financial support and use is missing. The typical financial instrument is some form of tax, so the basis of financial contribution is not personal use or benefit but more likely the governmental area in which you live, the size of your taxable income or the pattern of your expenditures. In OECD countries at the start of the eighties, 33 per cent of tax revenues came from personal incomes, 8 per cent from corporate incomes, 24 per cent from social security charges, 5 per cent from property taxes and 29 per cent from expenditure on goods and services (Lloyds Bank, 1982, Table 2).

For expository purposes it is sometimes convenient to present market and bureaucratic regimes as polarised options. There are courses financed entirely out of user charges. Other courses are totally tax- financed, with no fees and no uncompensated loss of earnings or of leisure time by learners. But, in practice, there are far more regimes of mixed financing. Courses are often part-financed out of taxation, or at least assisted through tax concessions. Many courses have a tuition fee, and there is also an implicit price to be paid by the learner, a time price which can be approximately converted into earn- ings or leisure foregone. So there is a market element in their finan- cing. Learners have to make some financial contribution and a commit- ment of some of their valuable time. These explicit and implicit user charges may not even account for the bulk of total revenue and of total resources for the courses. But they may create the degree of sensitivity of suppliers to the wishes of learners which is one of the alleged advantages of market regimes.

It is necessary to examine the characteristics of mixed financing re- gimes as well as the characteristics of purely market and purely bureaucratic allocation. For some types of adult education, e.g. for very low income or very severely handicapped adults, there might be little or no provision without a high degree of tax financing. But for many kinds of provision the degree to which financial costs are met out of taxes or from user charges is a more open choice. It is a choice which will be influenced by a number of factors. The consequences of a chosen subsidy-and-price regime for the magnitude and incident of costs and benefits will be one set of factors. The way in which users and suppliers of instructional services respond to changes in critical variables like prices, incomes and preferences is another.

MARKET, BUREAUCRATIC AND MIXED REGIMES

Market-financing

Perhaps the greatest attraction of the market, as the predominant financing mechanism, is its potential capacity for decentralising control over the allocation of resources. A major share in this control is accorded to individuals, using their own definition of what they need to learn. Their definition of need is given effective expression by ensuring that the pattern, quality and amount of provision is largely determined by what they are willing to pay for.

As Griffith points out (1978, p.390), the survival of proprietary schools in the United States depends upon their ability to keep developing programmes which are exactly responsive to the felt needs of would-be learners, and to satisfy those needs in the quickest possible time. They face fierce competition, not only from each other, but from community colleges and public technical institutes offering similar programmes at lower or even at zero fees (see Breneman and Nelson, 1981). Poor communications (high information costs for the would-be learner) and alienation from the educational culture of postsecondary public institutions deter some adults. To the extent that proprietary schools can do better than public institutions in gearing curriculum and teaching methods more precisely to felt needs they may overcome, for a while, the fee advantage of public sector institutions. In the United Kingdom also, there is a considerable sector of independent, mainly for-profit, postsecondary institutions below the level of higher education. They fill some of the gaps in provision left by public institutions unresponsive to felt needs; or they succeed in selling similar courses at higher fees because they are better able to offer what adults want (see Williams and Woodhall, 1979).

Griffith (1978) makes an important distinction between learning needs which are defined by adults themselves, and their needs defined by someone else. When adults are looking for some particular help in order to acquire skills or knowledge these are felt needs. When suppliers satisfy these felt needs, the learners reveal their needs by providing funds for what they want and by participating in an educational activity. This quid pro quo, mainly in return for satisfaction of wants, is the essence of the market relationship. Griffith contrasts learner-defined need with expert-defined need. Designated experts identify a desirable standard and measure total need as the difference between observed and desired levels of provision. Experts decide 'what is to be learned by whom, for what purposes, and under what conditions' (Griffith, 1978, p. 384).

Would-be learners and experts both use value positions in defining needs and setting priorities. As long as collusion between suppliers can be prevented, it is possible for market financing to award the predominant power to implement their definition of need to those learners with sufficient disposable income to pay full-cost fees. Vouchers or entitlements, cashable into tax funds by suppliers, can be used to give this power to all adults, irrespective of their disposable incomes. Under a market regime resource allocation is demand-led. Those who feel the need for education, want it and can pay for it – with money or vouchers – may be described as demanding it. Some will demand it who do not, according to experts, need it; and others who are thought by experts to need it, may not want it. For most practical purposes, demand can be regarded as a subset of felt need. Not all felt need for learning converts into demand because our wants characteristically exceed our capacity to satisfy them in full and simultaneously. The complexity of the process by which a felt need to learn is translated into an effective demand for educational services is underlined by the fact that demand is demand at a series of prices. At different prices we would pay for different qualities and quantities of services. The would-be learner orders his educational and non-educational wants by relating them, weighted by their respective prices, to each other. His ordering reflects not only his relative valuation of different needs, but also his relating of these needs to the prices he faces and to the income he has at his disposal.

The diffusion of power over the allocation of resources to and within education, and a strong indirect role in determining provision, is attractive to many would-be learners among the adult population.

It also attracts those reformers who wish to combine centralised functions like planning and research with strong grassroots development at the local level and diversity of offerings (e.g. Edding, 1981). One argument for market financing is that it promotes local initiatives and institutional adaptability compared with the central co-ordination and tendency to institutional inertia which often characterises bureaucratic allocation.

There is some evidence that certain kinds of educational services for adults are what Hirschman (1970) calls a 'connoisseur good'. This is a good where a quality decline can be conceived as a price increase, and these equivalent price increases are different for different customers. Appreciation of the quality of the same provision differs widely between adults. A quality decline inflicts very different losses — different equivalent price increases — on different customers. Hirchman argues (1970, pp.138-139) that, as long as consumer incomes are not too dissimilar, these equivalent prices are positively correlated with corresponding consumer surpluses. A consumer surplus is the difference between the price a consumer would pay for a good or service and the price he _does_ pay.

This argument is important for several reasons. Traditional economic analysis is conducted in terms of quantity and price, which is quite appropriate for analysing the demand for a bland, homogenised product like petrol of a given octane rating. Customers cannot detect quality differences between petrol offered by competing companies. A change in quality, to another grade of petrol, changes the equivalent price in the same way for all customers, which is the opposite of the situation with a connoisseur good like education. Where customer perceptions of the same service differ widely, as is the case in education, it is important to explore the role of quality change as well as of price change. To some extent, this can be done through the device of expressing quality change as an equivalent price change. The essential point is that an equivalent price change varies from customer to customer. Moreover, those who are relatively insensitive to a money price change may be very sensitive to a decline in quality: '... someone who had a very high consumer surplus before deterioration precisely because he is a connoisseur and would be willing to pay, say, twice the actual price of the article at its original quality, may drop out as a customer as soon as the quality deteriorates provided a non-deteriorated competing product is available, be it at a much higher price'. (Hirschman, 1970, p.49).

In a market regime these complicated assessments of financial price, quality and quantity of educational services, traded-off against the same dimensions of non-educational services, can be devolved to the would-be learner. Market financing may provide the customer with an exit option, the chance to stop buying one service and to patronise another; or the option to express loyalty by continuing to buy a service. He translates a judgement about quality and money price into exit or loyalty. When people protest that a service is not meeting their felt needs they are taking what Hirschman calls the voice option. Exit/loyalty and voice are respectively market and non-market forces, economic and political tactics available to the adult in search of resources to aid his learning. In practice, adults can exercise both options in a complementary fashion. They do not have to choose between them. It is the enthusiasts for competing financing regimes who have pretended that market and non-market systems of financing are bound to be mutually exclusive :
'... both laissez-faire and interventionist doctrines have looked at market and non-market forces in a strictly Manichaean way, it being understood that the laissez-faire advocate's forces of good are the interventionist's forces of evil and vice versa.' (Hirschman, 1970, p.19).

It is probably fair comment by Hirschman (1970, p.17) that many economists not only favour the exit option but are prejudiced against voice, which seems to be a messy, personal and cumbersome mode of expressing dissatisfaction compared with the neat and direct anonymity of voting for (loyalty) or against (exit) in the marketplace. The argument is that the customer whose needs are not being satisfied by suppliers shifts his custom and funds from one supplier to another. In doing so he improves his own welfare, as he defines it, but also that of the whole society: suppliers are forced to attend to the wishes of customers or be starved of funds.

Hirschman advances another thesis which is of particular relevance to adult education. This is the thesis that the typical market mechanism and the typical political mechanism can work side by side either in mutually supportive harmony or perpetually undercutting each other's effectiveness. The availability of the exit option may sharply reduce the probability that the voice option will be used effectively. This has been a favourite contention of those who oppose the existence of market-financed private schools in the United Kingdom; and it could be used to oppose essentially market-type instruments such as educational entitlements for adults. However, in defining educational needs and resourcing programmes, the market can be a complement to rather than a rival of the political mechanism. When, in the late seventies, the price of many supposedly avocational programmes in British adult education were raised high and fast, neither the participation rate nor the composition of the clientele changed as much as the price, although the price change was often very large when adjusted for hidden quantity changes due to reduced course lengths. Until that time many of the clients had certainly been enjoying a consumer surplus. Market financing, which transfers funds direct from households or enterprises to suppliers, became much more important. As a result, the exit option has become a far more powerful sanction available to customers. The voice option had been effective mainly in protecting the financial interest of better-off and better-educated adults. It has become less significant. To the extent that there are positive externalities from such programmes, these can still be pursued by selective subsidy. Intervention by regulation or by subsidy can alter the pattern of supply and of consumption of educational services from what it would be under total market financing, i.e. where paying customers are the only definers of educational needs.

Publicly-provided or privately-provided and publicly-subsidised services can always enjoy a money price advantage over private sector provision financed exclusively through the market. But customers choose on the basis of expected quantity and quality of outcomes, as well as on price. It is not price along but the ratio of price to quality and quantity which matters for the would-be learner. If adults perceive that what is being offered in tax-financed and market-financed institutions is sufficiently different as to be non-competitive, then price competition between the two is illusory. There can only be price competition when customers believe that they are comparing money prices of essentially the same services from rival suppliers. The suppliers of cheaper services can lose custom to higher-price suppliers if they reduce quality further and have some customers who are more quality conscious than the rest. Since quality consciousness if often at least as important a demand factor as price per unit of quantity, it is to be expected that, even if disposable incomes were equal, high quality/high price suppliers would co-exist with lower quality/lower price suppliers. If disposable incomes are not equal, even greater variation in the quality and price of offerings can be expected in order to cater for all tastes and all purses.

The principal arguments against financing through a private for-profit market are economic, the presence of externalities, and social, the

effects of income inequalities and of variations in tastes and values.
The economic argument has extra power in the case of adult education
because of the importance of time prices for adult learners. As with
health services, the importance of the time price considerably
diminishes the attraction of an allocative mechanism which is sensitive
to money prices. Three key features of the demand for adult education
services are shared with the demand for health services (on which see
Williams, 1974). The first feature is the fact that the time price which
has to be paid by the adult learner is not received by the supplier of
resources in aid of learning. A price which is paid but not received
cannot fulfil the informational role of a money price. Secondly, the
distribution of time resources between individuals is not identical to the
distribution of money resources, and the pattern of demand will be
influenced by both. Thirdly, the money value of time often differs significantly from person to person. Consequently, an educational offering
with a constant time price implies large differences from person to
person in the money equivalent of that time price. For all these
reasons allocative mechanisms responding to price-directed money flows
will be sensitive to the felt needs of would-be learners only in a highly
biased fashion which is liable to misinform suppliers about those needs.

The literature of economics concentrates heavily on the inability of the
market to finance an optimal supply of a good or service which has
considerable externalities. In other words, the objection to the market
is in terms of its effect (1) on the supply of such services and (2) on
the magnitude and distribution of benefits. Far less attention is given
to the weakness of the market as a financing mechanism for a service
where demand is heterogeneous and heavily skewed by implicit costs for
the same service, costs which vary wildly from person to person. In
adult education the implicit cost of learner time is generally a larger
proportion of explicit plus implicit cost — the total price to be paid —
than it is in any other kind of education.

The value of learner time is highly variable for two main reasons. The
first is due to long term changes. In the United Kingdom, over decades,
male activity rates have tended to fall and female activity rates to rise.
The proportion of the labour force working a standard week or more has
tended to fall. About one quarter now work less than a standard week.
During the whole twentieth century average actual hours of paid work in
the United Kingdom have fallen from around 60 hours per week to around
40 hours per week. As the number of paid hours of work per week falls,
non-paid work time tends to become less scarce — only if it is assumed

that demands on such time remain constant can we be certain that it is becoming less scarce. For many individuals the time price of non-paid work and of leisure has tended to fall (unevenly), even though unevenly rising labour productivity increases the price of foregoing paid work-time at the margin.

The second reason that the value of learner time is so variable is that the individual adult, living within this changing society and economy, is a changing person. People's valuations of competing uses of their own time vary over time; and one person's valuation may differ from another person's at any one point in time. The market operates with money paid and money received. Time price heavily influences a person's willingness to take up learning opportunities, but not in constant propor-tion to money price. Since this price is paid but not received, it does not influence the supplier. Left to its own devices, a market is bound to be an eccentric allocator of resources whenever the time price is a large proportion of total price. Resources cannot be geared closely to consumer preferences when the main information carrier, price, is partially disabled. Only the money price, a varying proportion of the total price paid by the adult learner, is received by the supplier and enables him to purchase resources. Only that part of the total price influences directly the level and pattern of provision in a market regime. The non-money part of the total price influences the commitment of resources only from the demand side, skewing the level and pattern of take-up of learning opportunities.

The key to understanding why a given set of financing arrangements has the educational and distributive consequences it does have lies in re-actions to the costs of adult education. For the would-be learner these are reactions to non-money as well as to money costs. Patterns of take-up — who learns what — are the result of prices paid, those which are received and those which are not received.

Bureaucratic financing

The failings of markets as allocative mechanisms are frequently treated as arguments for state intervention by means of tax-financing (see Chapter 3). There are groups of adults who tend to do very badly under market arrangements. There is no incentive for employers to pay to train the unemployed, and the unemployed lack the income or savings to pay for training themselves. Such adults tend to receive no training if their training is left entirely to the market. In addition, there will tend to be under-investment in training wherever there are important spill-over benefits from training. In other words, the level and distribution of training tends to be socially suboptimal, in terms of equity or efficiency, with respect to some groups of adults and some types of skills.

However, it would be a mistake to think that the case for tax-financing and bureaucratic control of adult education rests entirely on the failings of the market as an economically efficient or socially acceptable finan-cing mechanism. As Weisbrod (1978, p.134) points out, the government sector (from tax finance) and the voluntary sector (from donations and tax concessions) enjoy an important measure of independence from customers. Because of what he calls their 'non-quid pro quo revenues' they have a discretionary power over their output which competitive pressures tend to deny to enterprises or to for-profit educational insti-tutions. Armed with this financial independence, governments can engage in social engineering through education. One form of this engineering is Plato in modern dress, a technocratic paternalism which identifies and resources education appropriate to the 'real' needs of adults rather than their felt needs. Equipped with tax funds, techno-crats can take advantage of the falling costs of financing recurrent education to deploy educational programmes and combat skill obsolescence, unemployment and any other social bads (see Peston 1979, 1981). A dif-ferent kind of social engineering is designed to counteract the institutional imperfections which characterise market-based provision. Whenever suppliers enjoy preponderant market power they may be tempted to make prices, accumulate profits or create institutional empires at the expense of the learner and his definition of need. Public monitoring and inter-vention to counter anti-competitive market practices, and to protect the interests of learners, are essential. Indeed, the entire structure of learning opportunities facing adults might be overhauled. The objective is to design compensatory actions which will reduce imperfections and give greater choice to individuals than they would enjoy under unregula-ted market provision (see Glennerster, 1981; ACACE, 1982).

Even if all educational services were provided by public institutions and financed to offer instruction at zero tuition price, there would still be important elements of a market relationship in transactions between institutional supplier and would-be learner. When an adult seeks resources to assist her learning, there is always a time price to be paid if the learner is to inform herself accurately and fully about the benefits to be gained, as well as a time price in studying. Improvements in educational technology may help to reduce such prices. But search and study costs cannot be abolished. They have to be borne by the household or by the enterprise. Governments may intervene to offset such costs, possibly with a money payment which the would-be learner regards as compensation for the next-best alternative use of the time which is foregone during search and study. From adult to adult this time price varies as greatly as the equivalent price resulting from changing the quality of provision of a connoisseur good. The reason for this variation is that the magnitude of the time price depends directly upon the nature and valuation of the next-best use of time for each person. For many adults, the demand for education depends as heavily or more heavily upon this implicit, non-money price than it does upon any money price. The flow of resources into adult education and its distribution therein, is sensitive to individual demand, so government interventions to reduce or offset time prices can powerfully influence who learns what.

However, bureaucratic allocation is not automatically more efficient, and socially more acceptable, than a defective market mechanism. If bureaucracies try to operate entirely without money prices their own weakness as information systems becomes particularly glaring. They tend not to be as good as actual markets at generating information about consumer preferences, product quality and production technology. They tend not to be as good at communicating complicated messages about preferences, qualities and costs; nor as good at creating incentives to suppliers to produce services efficiently and in conformity with consumer preferences.

A full-blooded money price system can fulfil three functions :

- it helps to allocate resources between educational and non-educational uses, and between rival educational uses, according to the preferences of those who pay;

- it provides incentives to internal efficiency, since the payer has a keen interest in the quid pro quo, and the supplier must compete on price and quality in order to earn his own income;

- it informs buyers and sellers of the overall balance between demand and supply, and signals the investments required to meet future demand.

All these are functions which can be fulfilled without a price system. Resources can be allocated by central planners. Services can be rationed by queuing (according to the private opportunity cost of time) or using criteria like previous credentials, age, sex, occupation or any other individual traits. Internal efficiency can be pursued by setting norms for resourcing, such as staffing ratios, and gathering information on skill shortages and surpluses. But, in general, the record of bureaucracies in OECD countries does not suggest any automatic superiority of bureaucratic over market systems.

It has long been argued (e.g. Schultz, 1972, p.26) that government subsidies which reduce the money price of education to individuals frequently increase private demand at the expense of social efficiency. As provision is expanded, subsidised services tend increasingly to be provided well below cost, to people who have the income and would be willing to pay the full cost: there is a growing consumer surplus among the better-off adults. Since tax funds have alternative public uses, subsidising more and more education for the better-off is not necessarily socially efficient. Most tax funding is central funding, and in developed countries central governments, with one or two notable exceptions, have a poor record of spending on adult education. In part, this is because adult education is not always well placed to win in the fierce competition for public funds. It may do better in a multitude of budget battles scattered through a country's enterprises, voluntary organisations and households than it does in the Ministry of Finance. In part, this may be because tax funds tend to have benefited disproportionately the better-educated citizens, however much that contradicts a country's political rhetoric. It has taken the recurrence of massive unemployed in developed countries to begin to shift centrally-budgeted funds away from the better-off and towards poorer and more disadvantaged adults.

However, in Britain and many other developed countries, governments persist with perverse financing arrangements, i.e. arrangements which are patently inefficient, inequitable or both. Glennerster (1981, p.553) has argued that recent interest in adults shown by Ministries of Education and higher education institutions is consistent with the model of bureaucratic and professional self-interest used by Niskanen to explain budget strategies (see Niskanen, 1971 and DES, 1980). Glennerster lists a series of imperfections in British institutional arrangements. Some of these, such as the capital market, are seriously defective parts of the market mechanism judged as a financing arrangement. But some of the other imperfections in Glennerster's catalogue are arguably the consequence of government action or inaction rather than market failure. He cites financing arrangements which favour a 'front-loaded' education system; the culture of schools which misinforms young people and the culture of the workplace constraining the use of time in and around paid work time; financial incentives to public institutions to favour full aginst part-time teaching; and 'arbitrary administrative divisions between categories of income maintenance provided by the State which prevent individuals exercising a rational choice between work, education, retirement and leisure' (Glennerster, 1981, p.555). Governments have their own failings; and their capacity to correct those of the private market in pursuit of social goals is often quite limited in practice. Weisbrod (1978, p.1) was making a similar point when he argued that governmental capacity to fulfil the corrective function suffers from a double handicap. Government information about consumer demands is as limited and biased, if differently so, as that of private decision-makers. Moreover, in government incentives 'rarely coincide with what is required to correct the private market's failures, for government officials can be expected to act not according to some abstract concepts of allocative efficiency and distributional equity but according to some self-interest model'.

Institutions or individuals may ruin the potential of bureaucratic financing as a means of achieving public goals. Institutions have a habit of interposing their own goals between public policy and the adult learner, and never more so than in the way they manage cross-subsidisation between groups of learners. Simple pricing rules, such as zero pricing on all tax-financed courses, can rarely be adopted. The most likely consequence of such a rule is indiscriminate and arbitrary subsidies to some adults (learners) from other adults (taxpayers) which accord ill with public equity goals. On the other hand, complex tariffs can facilitate the pursuit of institutional goals such as maximising the growth of the institution's budget, or of its staff, or the salaries of the directorate, or its status. The suppression of competitive market pressures by means of a rule-bound and monolithic system of public provision may lead to insensitivity to the felt needs of groups of adults and the use of high-cost methods when lower-cost methods are available. It may lead to a producer-dominated system. Competitive pressures can lead to cartels at the expense of the customer, or to a disregard of beneficial spillovers and exclusive concentration on the satisfaction of private wants. In other words, both the absence and the presence of competitive market forces can lead to social inefficiency. Neither in public ownership nor in the market is there a ready panacea. Under either regime, if suppliers are price-makers and enjoy dominating market power they may use resources at lower efficiencies and disregard the wishes of many adults.

For economists, the attraction of the market as an allocative mechanism
has always been its capacity to provide a massively detailed and sensi-
tively interdependent system of costed options to demanders and
suppliers. It is a system which can be made sensitive to changes in
underlying preferences and to the resultant revaluations by suppliers and
demanders, or to technological change and its cost consequences. Such
changes are reflected in amounts supplied to and demanded from the
market, or in a veritable chain of price and quantity adjustments. The
pathological conditions which afflict markets (imperfections), and
inherent malfunctioning with respect to externalities (market failure),
do reduce their sensitivity to changes in preferences and technology.
Their allocative efficiency is diminished. In order to function at all,
markets require government intervention to establish and maintain a
framework of property rights. Beyond that prerequisite, market-
improving interventions may be limited to removing or reducing some
imperfections, for example by improving the knowledge of would-be
learners or facilitating the entry of new suppliers of instructional
services. Interventions may be more radical. The distribution of educational purchasing power may be altered by issuing entitlements and
attempting to influence preferences, or by using institutional subsidies
to alter the cost structures of suppliers. Both levels of intervention
leave the essential operations of the market intact but change the outcome. More radical still is the creation of a deliberate, state-
controlled imperfection like state monopoly supply, or the introduction
of state price fixing to operate directly on the entire signalling system
of the market, and on its sensitivity to preferences and to costs. The
practice of OECD countries offers examples of all three levels of state
intervention in the workings of the market.

Mixed regimes

Although most actual financing regimes combine features of markets and
of bureaucracies, this does not diminish the importance of the essential
differences between the two kinds of allocative mechanism. In mixed
financing regimes it is not fixed and pre-determined who will allocate
funds, whereas a true market regime accords this power to those who
benefit from and can pay for education. Under a market regime opportunities are open only to those who can pay. Government interventions
characteristically make opportunities available according to some notion
of need and irrespective of payment by those in need. Education available through the market is paid for only by those who benefit from it and
can pay for it. Government intervention introduces funding from tax

monies, sometimes using the criterion of ability to pay among all adults, irrespective of their use of educational services. In other words, the locus of power over the allocation of funds, and the incidence of educational benefits and costs, vary as between a market regime and one in which there is substantial government intervention to supplement or displace market arrangements, i.e. a mixed regime.

It is one of the advantages of Marxian economics that the distribution and deployment of power in society is a main agenda item instead of being left implicit, as it is in bourgeois (neoclassical) economics (see Lindbeck, 1971; Carnoy and Levin, 1976; Vinokur, 1980; Apple, 1982). The disadvantage is that the Marxian analysis is bound to remain partial and predictable because it is fundamentally incapable of development, except in an exegetical sense. This is unfortunate because financing arrangements can be very revealing of the distribution of power within a country. Despite Marxist writings, there is an analysis which is effectively missing from the literature. This is a convincing analysis which — to paraphrase Samuel Bowles — views the output of adult education not as a distribution of skills embodied in individuals (human capital) but as a distribution of power. In order to maintain credibility some radical economists find it necessary to abandon the state of Marx and Engels — 'a committee for managing the common affairs of the whole bourgeoisie' — and to use essentially non-Marxist models such as the state as 'an arena in which class alliances are formed' (Bowles, 1980, p. 208).

In a state of shifting coalitions it is far easier to explain, ex post facto, mixed systems of financing, for services like adult education, which have evolved over many years. These systems represent the residual of many ad hoc compromises between those defending their own property rights and those seeking to enjoy the property of others. During the seventies OECD countries traded-off labour productivity increases for jobs and associated vocational learning opportunities: four million new service jobs in the European Community 1973-79; thirteen million new jobs in the decade in the United States, mostly in services. But by 1982 registered unemployment had reached nearly 30 million in all OECD countries, of which 11 million were in the European Community and another 11 million in the United States. According to OECD, unemployment in its two dozen member countries cost $340 billion of lost output in 1981, which equalled the combined gross domestic products of Canada and Denmark.

In the United Kingdom alone, the fiscal cost (benefit payments plus tax revenues foregone) of each unemployed person by the end of 1982 was averaging about £4,500 a year (MSC 1982, p.4). So the 3.3 million registered unemployed were costing the national exchequer some £14.85 billion a year, which was far in excess of public spending on the education and training of adults. The implied share-out of paid work and income between the 10 per cent of OECD workers who were unemployed and the 90 per cent who were employed is the outcome of a complex power struggle. This continuing struggle is a major determinant of the level and distribution of learning opportunities for adults in OECD countries. The level of economic activity and the distribution of paid work between all job-seekers in the paid economy are major determinants of the demand for training. In so far as they affect the level and pattern of economic activity, public policy decisions on employment, economic growth and inflation are likely to influence the availability of vocational learning opportunities for adults. The eighties could witness a decrease in vocational learning opportunities as dramatic as the new employment-based increase of the seventies. All that is required is a slight shift in the delicate balance of power between the groups who command the levers of public policy, giving a lower priority to employment and to public spending on education and training.

The two major options available to most OECD countries are (1) expanding output, and thereby slowing down, or occasionally reversing, the reduction in the number of jobs and vocational learning opportunities; and (2) increasing the number of jobs and learning opportunities by accelerating and making more comprehensive existing trends towards sub-division of jobs and reduction in hours per job. Of course, the two options can be pursued simultaneously; and success with the first would help to pay for the increased cost of training per hour of paid work which is implied in the second.

Macroeconomic policies have profound and wide-ranging implications for the demand for training and capacity to finance it. So does the way in which governments intervene to influence the application of new technologies. It is estimated that over the next two decades the impact of the micro-chip, if it is applied, is likely to put at risk between one and two-thirds of all existing-size jobs, i.e. 35 to 70 million jobs in either of the equally large European Community or United States workforces (Merritt, 1982, p.74). What happens to existing vocational learning opportunities when existing office technology is applied to 15 million clerical or 5 million bank jobs in the European Community? The traditional risk groups — women, ethnic minorities, the disabled and the unskilled — are unlikely to suffer from technological change as heavily as skilled workers in offices or factories. The unskilled and the 'knowledge class' may survive best. It is tradesmen and typists who are most at risk. An example of the immediate training implications of technological change comes from the ITT company Standard Electric Lorenz:

> 'In switching over to electronic telex machine production it replaced 936 parts in the electromechanical version with a single micro-processor, and at the same time transformed its own shopfloor. Jobs requiring training dropped from 82 per cent to just 35 per cent, semi-skilled ones that had only been 15 per cent rose to 35 per cent and at the highly skilled end, men in white coats, it jumped from two per cent to 30 per cent.' (Merritt, 1982, p. 72).

There is a division between pluralists, who search for mechanisms to reconcile individual preferences and actions, and statists, who accord an overriding will to one collective, which is called 'the State' but is actually central government. Economist members of the first group tend to prefer market mechanisms, although some are puzzling over the actual and preferred properties of mechanisms for public choice (see Mueller, 1979). Economist members of the second group concentrate more on the technical problems of putting into effect the will of a benevolent government. For members of this group recurrent education is really 'the next stage of social policy' and its finance is characterised as 'merely a part of general public finance, of who is willing to pay for what' (Peston, 1981, p. 548). However, one of the most obvious features of public finance is that people are forced to pay for things whether they are willing or not.

It may be less confusing to recognise that markets and bureaucracies are the characteristic financing and allocative mechanisms for two different varieties of educational planning. These can be called market and non-market planning, or decentralised and centralised planning. The market mechanism is a planning device by which economic agents — members of households, enterprises, parafiscs, central and local government — exchange information and co-ordinate their behaviour, as suppliers and users of educational services, in response to impersonal price signals and judgements of quality. By contrast, where non-market planning is dominant, the visible hand of government overrules the invisible hand of the market in order to manage the supply of services

according to a different set of priorities than those which are implied
in the net effect of the decisions of the economic agents. Non-market
or central planning is usually dominated by supply-side thinking.
Equipped with tax funds, governments concentrate on altering the provision of learning opportunities, in quantity, quality and distribution,
from that which obtains when all funds for provision come through the
market. If markets can be made to work well, the customer has a predominant voice in determining provision. If central planning works
well, government has the predominant voice, and the allocation of funds
may reflect government judgements about manpower requirements or
desirable cultural goals. Governments can manipulate demand with
financial carrots and sticks, and regulation of access to learning opportunities, though this is by no means easy since the individual choice
factors underlying the pattern and level of take-up of learning opportunities remain remarkably obscure and under-researched (see Harnqvist,
1978).

In practice, most allocative systems for adult education in OECD
countries exhibit a perpetual tension between market and non-market
planning tendencies. The tension may be creative or destructive. This
is nowhere more evident than in experience with pricing systems. Under
a regime of market financing the essence of the pricing system is differential payment for differential consumption. In a tax-financed regime of
bureaucratic allocation payment is not related to consumption: payment
is not necessarily the same for everyone, nor is consumption equal
between taxpayers, or between taxpayers and non-taxpayers (such as
non-residents). If services are divorced from the taxation which pays
for them there is a lack of direct connexion between payment and consumption in the minds of taxpayers and of beneficiaries. This can
produce severe difficulties. Zero-money pricing of tax-financed
services can eliminate market-financed substitutes. This may diminish
the total amount of resources flowing into educational provision because
all purchased resources then have to be competed away from the many
and powerful competitors for public funds. As rising taxation reduces
their disposable income, taxpayers tend to become more and more
resistant to an apparently insatiable demand for very expensive 'free'
public services. Zero-money pricing means that beneficiaries will
continue to demand more and more educational services up to the point
where the private gain from a further hour of education no longer exceeds
the gain from a further hour spent in some non-educational use of time.
The value of the adult's last hour of educational consumption may be
much less than the cost to the community of providing it 'free'. But the

adult has no incentive to curtail his consumption of these 'free' services as long as they yield satisfactions in excess of those from the next best competing use of his time (see Rowley, 1969, pp.174-175). The result is a chronic excess of demand for zero-money priced services over ability to tax-finance what is being demanded, and an inability to tap non-tax sources of funds if private suppliers have been competed out of existence. The excess of demand over supply has to be resolved by adulteration of quality or by non-money price rationing of demand, such as queuing, or relocation and rescheduling of courses, all devices using the differential private value of time. A different kind of solution to this dilemma is to use money prices even in the programmes of publicly-funded institutions. This will provide them with non-tax revenues and it will ration demand. It can be combined with selective funding of adult learners, in addition to public funding of programmes, and a public policy of promoting and regulating a healthy private sector (see Breneman and Nelson, 1981, Chapter 6).

In regimes of mixed financing the tax and market components can be used to modify each other. Tax-financing tends to produce supplier-dominated provision in which education is treated either as a collective good or as a merit good. Market-financing tends to produce demand-dominated provision, in which education is treated as a private good. The two regimes can be managed so that they improve each other. That is to say, features of one regime are grafted onto the other in order to remedy defects and alter outcomes in a direction which is defined as socially optimal. To improve the sensitivity of non-market or bureau-cratic allocation to needs other than those defined by government or by educational institutions, accountability devices are introduced — accountability meaning improved responsiveness of suppliers to users rather than to government. To remedy defects of the market system, devices are used to neutralise the effects of a given distribution of values in the population, e.g. price-reducing subsidies reflecting a merit good approach; or to neutralise a given distribution of income, e.g. educational entitlements or vouchers.

In many developed countries the trend in financing adult education and training has been to supplement rather than to displace the market as the dominant allocative mechanism. This is much easier said than done because it is so difficult to practice to control an incipient substitution of tax funds for market-based funds. As government steps forward employers and households tend to step back. Government must either draw back and risk the collapse of the educational provision it is sub-sidising, or continue to subsidise and find that private sector funds are gradually withdrawn, forcing government to increase tax-funding to maintain the level of provision. Where provision would not be market-funded anyway there is no problem. This is the case with provision for unemployed adults such as the Training Opportunities Scheme in the United Kingdom. Where the government intervenes by legal compulsion alone, as with safety training in the United Kingdom, the substitution problem is avoided. Where government intervenes with public subsidy as well as legal compulsion, as with safety training in Denmark, there is a danger of tax-for-price substitution.

An example: the pursuit of equity

It is extremely difficult to manage a mixed financing regime in pursuit of public goals. The pursuit of equity goals may be taken as an example. Difficulties begin with the notion of equity. The radical position is that the major equity goal of adult education is to alter the distribution of power within society. Unless that can be done, the liberal attempt to achieve greater equalisation of life chances between individuals of different ages, social classes and economic circumstances is doomed. It will not rise above ineffective and cosmetic tinkering.

The choice between radical and liberal positions is presented as a choice between a wholesale re-engineering of society and micro-level adjustments to the circumstances of one person in relation to another. The feasibility of these competing conceptions of equity should be examined. Public power can be used to make some discrete adjustments to the life chances of individuals within existing societies, using a mix of educational and other forms of social engineering. The Scandinavian democracies provide good examples of sustained efforts of this type. The feasibility of the radical concept of equity, as an educational objective, is, in its own terms, more doubtful. At best, it is a moot point whether educational systems can have significant leverage on the overall distribution of power within societies. Indeed, the Marxian analysis, which is the principal source of the radical concept of equity, cannot treat education as an 'exogenous policy instrument' (see Bowles, 1980). Education is bound to reinforce existing distributions of power because the education system is a dependency of the economic and class structure of society. Education systems are limited to a fundamentally passive or, at best, co-operative role in society — the correspondence principle. Theirs is not an active and initiating role (see Carnoy and Levin, 1976).

Those who do not wholeheartedly subscribe to the Marxian analysis may yet accept that, in any conceivable political regime, the menu of individual choices is bound to be more or less constrained by power distributions which are embodied in the institutional structures of society. The extent to which these distributions and structures will tolerate deliberate alterations in the life chances of individual citizens is always difficult to predict. However, the record is not generally encouraging in developed countries. Equity objectives are essentially directional. That is to say, they indicate the direction which change needs to take for it to be regarded as an improvement on the present situation. Most economists are sceptical about the efficiency of educational programming in achieving equity goals. They also doubt whether greater equalisation of educational outcomes, if it could be achieved, would produce very much progress towards income redistribution. In the United States, Sweden and the United Kingdom the most common view is that the best chance of achieving that goal lies by the direct route: redistribute income (see Rivlin, 1975; Fagerlind, 1975; Jencks, 1979; Le Grand, 1982).

In the United Kingdom the richest fifth of the income distribution has for years enjoyed at least three times as much public education spending as the poorest fifth. Members of the professions and managers generally have far more spent on their education than semiskilled or unskilled workers. Inequalities of spending and inequalities of outcome have changed little in recent decades. On only one measure, the dispersion of earnings, has there been a real tendency for inequalities to lessen during the twentieth century, and it is not clear whether or to what extent this can be attributed to the expansion of educational provision over the same period. Le Grand (1982, p. 77) baldly concludes: 'Overall it seems that public expenditure on education has failed as a means of achieving equality'. In order to increase equality he even argues a strong case for reducing public subsidies to education after school leaving age, although it has to be noted that he seems to be considering chiefly the expensive post-compulsory initial education which is so unevenly distributed in Britain, rather than post-initial education.

A weak specification of equity is equality of access, where individuals of similar ability have access to the same education, irrespective of their social and economic circumstances. This 'elite' specification is close to that of R.H. Tawney (quoted by Becker, 1975, p.123) when he argued that equality obtains:

'... in so far as, and only in so far as, each member of the
community, whatever his birth, or occupation, or social position,
possesses in fact, and not merely in form, equal chances of using
to the full his natural endowments of physique, of character, and
of intelligence. '

Such a specification recognises the inequality of personal gifts. It is a
major goal of those who specify equality in this way to engineer an
environment where 'earnings and investments would differ essentially
because of differences in capacities' (Becker, 1975, p.123). This is a
long way from attempting to equalise income or even educational spending per individual, although Becker (1975, p.124) hypothesises that to
pursue equal opportunity to be unequal would reduce inequalities in
educational investments and earnings between individuals. Even this
meritocratic version of equity requires extensive use of subsidies to
providers and to learners, and comprehensive regulation to enforce
criteria of access to learning resources which are free of all forms of
discrimination except for discrimination in favour of ability plus effort.

However, the range of possible equity goals is far wider than this, as
can be seen from Le Grand's (1982, p.74) formidable taxonomy of
possible specifications of equality:

'There seem to be four basic interpretations of the objective of
equality in the field of education: equality of use of the education
system; equality of the private cost per unit of use; equality of
public expenditure on education; and equality of outcome of
education, defined variously in terms of educational qualification,
occupation or earnings. Each of these may refer either to equality
between all individuals, between all individuals of the same ability
or between the average members of different social groups. '

To equalise access and use between all individuals of equal ability would
be difficult enough to achieve, although it is less difficult to move in
that direction. To equalise public spending, irrespective of ability,
which is an objective favoured by some proponents of educational entitlements, would require a sacrifice of some productivity. To move
towards greater equality of outcomes would require public investments
which differed widely from individual to individual, as they do now, but
using different criteria. There would have to be far less spending on
the most advantaged, and very much increased spending on those who
are most disadvantaged and handicapped by genetic, social and economic

circumstances: a massive extension of the principle underlying affirm-
ative action or positive discrimination policies. An even larger
sacrifice of productivity is implied in this version of equity.

Successively more radical specifications of equality, up to and including equality of outcomes, applied to larger and larger fractions of the
population require more and more massive public funding, taxation and
government intervention. Equity may be horizontal — between
individuals of the same generation; or vertical — between those of
different generations. Adult education policies have traditionally pursued both types of equity. In developed countries, younger members of
the workforce have usually had more spent on their initial formal
education than their seniors. They also enjoy a disproportionately large
share of paid educational leave (see Killeen and Bird, 1981). To make
significant inroads into that kind of intergenerational inequality would be
extraordinarily expensive. The reduction in the social rate of return
due to shortening of the benefit stream is usually argued against even
relatively short-term postponements of expensive formal education
after the end of initial education (see Stoikov, 1975). The same argument can be applied to any switching of resources away from the
education of younger towards older and older adults. It would be a
separate but no less formidable financial task to correct to any significant extent the gross inequalities of public and corporate spending
between those young adults who left school at the earliest legal moment
and those who enjoyed two to five years of further full-time education
end-on to compulsory schooling. The low base of public spending from
which any of these giant compensatory programmes would have to begin
can be gauged from the estimate that in 1976-77 gross public spending
per adult 25 years old and above in the United Kingdom was about £15,
i.e. 4 per cent of spending per head on those undergoing compulsory
schooling in the 5—15 year old age group (Drake, 1981, Table 2).

In addition to its magnitude, the problem is also one of instruments.
Collectivisation by itself is a fallible tool. It is sometimes argued that
privatisation of education provision means that payment for a service is
the same irrespective of the user's ability to pay:

> 'The real case for privatisation, here and elsewhere, is not a
> change in the actual allocation of output between different uses
> but mainly in the method of financing them. Privatisation
> increases the real inequality of incomes. This is necessarily
> all the greater the smaller is the range of services provided
> freely by the state and the larger is the range provided through
> the market.' (Kaldor, 1982).

Certainly, privatisation divorces the user's financial contribution from his ability to pay. But it does not follow that tax-financing can be trusted to produce greater equity. A change in the method of financing educational services does have a considerable effect on the allocation of output between different uses because the priorities of consumers under a market regime and of government under a bureaucratic one rarely coincide. There would be little point in supplementing the market with bureaucratic financing via tax and subsidy if the allocation of resources between educational and non-educational uses and the distribution of opportunities between persons remained unchanged. Further, the real inequality of incomes is not 'necessarily' greater the smaller is the range of services provided 'freely' by the state. If only things were that simple. This faith in the equitable consequences of 'free' subsidised services has repeatedly failed to survive exposure to evidence. Non-money price selection procedures have to replace price rationing, and these non-money price selection procedures almost invariably favour the most educated and those with high incomes (see Psacharopoulos, 1977). In real life, financing educational services out of tax funds and charging zero money prices may lead to greater inequality of real incomes than a mixed regime of subsidised but positive money prices and selective aid to students.

Any redistributive policy pursued through education has to succeed simultaneously on three levels. First, the non-money and the money price of learning facing the adult have to be reduced differentially, either by subsidising providers to reduce their costs and prices, or by enhancing learner incomes to enable them to afford the time price and pay full-cost money prices, or a mixture of these two tactics. Second, the curriculum, and thereafter the learning which results from combining learner time with other scarce resources, has to be altered from that which occurs without government intervention. Third, these changes have to be converted into alterations in the distribution between individuals of life chances and lifetime consumption profiles. The first level of redistribution, a price level, redistributes access to educational services. The second level is a redistribution of knowledge, skills and values, a shift in the pattern of what is learned and by whom. The third level of redistribution occurs to the extent that these price-induced learning gains by individuals are converted into real incomes. The knock-on effects from the level of access, to that of learning and to that of income are by no means automatic. Without sensitive and highly coordinated management of the structure of adult learning opportunities (access), of public and private sector suppliers of services (learning) and of labour market practices (incomes) a redistributive policy may not only fail: it may actually generate fresh inequalities.

REFERENCES

ADVISORY COUNCIL FOR ADULT AND CONTINUING EDUCATION
(1981), Protecting the future for adult education, Leicester

ADVISORY COUNCIL FOR ADULT AND CONTINUING EDUCATION
(1982), Continuing Education: From Policies to Practice, Leicester.

APPLE, Michael, W. (1982) Education and Power, Routledge and
Kegan Paul, London.

BAARS, W. S. (1979), Descriptions of the Vocational Training Systems:
Netherlands, European Centre for the Development of Vocational
Training, Berlin.

BARLOW, A. C. (1981), The Financing of Third Level Education, The
Economic and Social Research Institute, Dublin.

BECKER, G. S. (1975), Human Capital: a theoretical and empirical
analysis with special reference to education, 2nd edition, National
Bureau of Economic Research, New York.

BENDICK, M. Jr. (1977) 'Education as a Three Sector Industry' in
B. A. Weisbrod, The Voluntary Nonprofit Sector, Lexington Books,
Lexington, Mass.

BERG, I (1971), Education and Jobs: The Great Training Robbery,
Beacon Press, Boston.

BERTHOUD, R. (1978), Training Adults for Skilled Jobs: Skillcentre
Training and Local Labour Markets, Policy Studies Institute, London,
April.

BIRD, R. M. (1976), Charging for Public Services: A New Look at an
Old Idea, Canadian Tax Foundation, Toronto.

BLAUG, M. (1970), Introduction to the Economics of Education, Allen
Lane, The Penguin Press, London.

BLAUG, M. (1980), The Methodology of Economics or How Economists Explain, Cambridge University Press.

BLAUG, M. (1981), 'Comments on M. Peston and H. Glennerster' in Public Choice, 36, 3.

BOWLES, S. (1980), 'Education, Class Conflict and Uneven Development' in J. Simmons (ed.) The Education Dilemma, Pergamon Press, Oxford.

BOWLES, S. and GINTIS, H. (1976), Schooling in Capitalist America: Education Reform and the Contradictions of Economic Life, Routledge and Kegan Paul, London.

BRENEMAN, D.W. and NELSON, S.C. (1981), Financing Community Colleges: An Economic Perspective, The Brookings Institution, Washington DC.

BRIDGE, Gary, (1978), 'Information Imperfections: The Achilles' Heel of Entitlement Plans', School Review, 86, 3, May.

CARNOY, M. and LEVIN, H.M. (1976), The Limits of Educational Reform, Longman Inc., New York.

CENTRAL STATISTICAL OFFICE (1982), 'The effects of taxes and benefits on household income, 1980', Economic Trends, 339, January.

CLEMENT, Werner, (1979), Parafiscal Schemes for the Financing of Recurrent Education: Some Theoretical Considerations, Arbeitsheft Nr 8 des Instituts fur Sozialokonomie der Wirtschaftsuniversitat Wien, December.

CYERT, R.M. and MARCH, J.G. (1963), A Behavioural Theory of the Firm, Prentice Hall.

DEPARTMENT OF EDUCATION AND SCIENCE (1980), Continuing Education: Post-Experience Vocational Provision for Those in Employment: A Paper for Discussion, October.

DEPARTMENT OF EMPLOYMENT/MANPOWER SERVICES COMMISSION (1976), Training for Vital Skills: A Consultative Document, London.

DIAMOND COMMISSION (1979), Royal Commission on the Distribution of Income and Wealth, Report No. 7, Cmnd. 7595, Her Majesty's Stationery Office, London.

DOERINGER, P. and PIORE, M. (1971), Internal Labour Markets and Manpower Analysis, Heath, Lexington, Mass.

DORE, R. (1976), The Diploma Disease: Education, Qualification and Development, Allen and Unwin, London.

DOUGHERTY, C. R. S. (1972), 'Substitution and the Structure of the Labour Force', Economic Journal, March.

DRAKE, K. (1971). 'Explorations in Adult Education Costing I ', Research in Education, 6, November.

DRAKE, K. (1972), 'Explorations in Adult Education Costing II ', Research in Education, 7, May.

DRAKE, K. (1980), 'The United Kingdom' in Comparative study of the financial, legislative and regulatory structure of vocational training in the Federal Republic of Germany, France, Italy, the United Kingdom, European Centre for the Development of Vocational Training, Berlin.

DRAKE, K. (1981), 'Problems of financing an education system based on the concept of lifelong learning' in P. Himmelstrup, J. Robinson and D. Fielden (eds.) Strategies for Lifelong Learning I, University Centre of South Jutland, Denmark and the Association for Recurrent Education, United Kingdom, Esbjerg.

DRAKE, K. and RASMUSSEN, W. (1981), The Financing of Vocational Training in the European Community: Final Report on a Feasibility Study, European Centre for the Development of Vocational Training, Berlin (working paper).

EDDING, F. (1981), 'Economic Approaches to Recurrent Education' in M. Jourdan (ed.) Recurrent Education in Western Europe, National Foundation for Educational Research — Nelson Publishing Co. Ltd., London.

EIDE, K. (1981), 'Changing realities of work, leisure, education' in P. Himmelstrup, J. Robinson and D. Fielden (eds.) Strategies for Lifelong Learning I, University Centre of South Jutland, Denmark and the Association for Recurrent Education, United Kingdom, Esbjerg.

FAGERLIND, I. (1975), Formal Education and Adult Earnings, Almqvist and Wicksell International.

FOSTER, C.D., JACKMAN, R. and PERLMAN, M. (1980), Local Government Finance in a Unitary State, Allen and Unwin, London.

GHEZ, G.R. and BECKER, G.S. (1975), The Allocation of Time and Goods over the Life Cycle, National Bureau of Economic Research/ Columbia University Press, New York.

GLENNERSTER, H. (1981), 'The role of the state in financing recurrent education: lessons from European experience' in Public Choice, 36, 3.

GOLDTHORPE, J.H. et al. (1980), Social Mobility and Class Structure in Modern Britain, Clarendon Press, Oxford.

GOODMAN, Paul (1971), Compulsory Miseducation, Penguin Books, London.

GRIFFITH, William S. (1978), 'Educational Needs: Definition, Assessment and Utilisation', School Review, 86, 3, May

GROOMBRIDGE, B. (1981), 'Education and Disadvantaged Adults in the United Kingdom 1970-79' in Learning Opportunities for Adults, Volume 5: Widening Access for the Disadvantaged, Organisation for Economic Co-operation and Development, Paris.

HALSEY, A.H. et al. (1980), Origins and Destinations, Clarendon Press, Oxford.

HARNQVIST, K. (1978), Individual Demand for Education: Analytical Report, Organisation for Economic Co-operation and Development, Paris.

HARTLEY, K. (1974), 'Industrial Training and Public Policy: From Industrial Training Boards to the State Manpower Bank' in A.J. Culyer (ed.) Economic Policies and Social Goals, Martin Robertson, London.

HECLO, H. and WILDAVSKY (1981), The Private Government of Public Money, 2nd edition, Macmillan, London.

HIRSCH, F. (1977), The Social Limits to Growth, Routledge and Kegan Paul, London.

HIRSCHMAN, A. O. (1970), Exit, Voice and Loyalty: responses to decline in firms, organizations and states, Harvard University Press, Cambridge, Mass.

ILLICH, Ivan (1970), Deschooling Society, Harper and Row, New York.

INTERNATIONAL LABOUR OFFICE (1979) Ten Years of Training: Developments in France, Federal Republic of Germany and the United Kingdom 1968-78, Geneva.

JENCKS, C. et al. (1979), Who Gets Ahead? The Determinants of Economic Success in America, Basic Books.

JOHNSON, R. (1979) 'Education and Training in the 80s 'Employment Gazette, November.

KALDOR, Professor Lord (1982), Letter to The Times, October 6, p. 13.

KIDD, J. Roby (1962), Financing Continuing Education, Scarecrow Press, New York.

KILLEEN, J. and BIRD, M. (1981), Education and Work: a study of paid educational leave in England and Wales 1976/77, National Institute of Adult Education (England and Wales), Leicester.

KURLAND, Norman, D. (ed.) (1977), Entitlement Studies, National Institute of Education Papers in Education and Work No. 4, Washington DC.

LAWRENCE, D.H. (1950), Letter to Edward Garnett, 17.4.13 in Selected Letters, Penguin Books.

LAYARD, P.R.G., SARGAN, J.D., AGER, M.E. and JONES, D.J. (1971), Qualified Manpower and Economic Performance: An Inter-Plant Study in the Electrical Generating Industry, Allen Lane, the Penguin Press, London.

LE FIGARO (1982), Vendredi, 10 Septembre, Edition de 5 heures.

LE GRAND, J. (1982), Strategy for Equality: Redistribution and the Social Services, Allen and Unwin, London.

LEGAVE, Catherine and VIGNAUD, Dominique (1979), Descriptions of the Vocational Training Systems: France, European Centre for the Development of Vocational Training, Berlin.

LESLIE, Larry, L. (1978), 'Tax Allowances for Non-traditional Students', School Review, 86, 3, May.

LEVIN, Henry, M. (1976), 'Concepts of Economic Efficiency and Educational Production' in J.T. Froomkin and R. Radner (eds.) Education as an Industry, Ballinger, Cambridge, Mass.

LLOYDS BANK ECONOMIC BULLETIN (1982), 46, October.

LOCAL GOVERNMENT FINANCIAL STATISTICS, ENGLAND AND WALES, 1974-75, (1978), Her Majesty's Stationery Office, London.

LOCAL GOVERNMENT FINANCIAL STATISTICS, ENGLAND AND WALES, 1979-80, (1981), Her Majesty's Stationery Office, London.

LINDBECK, Assar (1971), The Political Economy of the New Left: An Outsider's View, Harper and Row, New York.

MACHLUP, F. (1962), The Production and Distribution of Knowledge in the United States, Princeton University Press, Princeton, New Jersey.

MACHLUP, F. (1980), Knowledge: Its Creation, Distribution and Economic Significance, Volume 1: Knowledge and Knowledge Production, Princeton University Press, Princeton, New Jersey.

MAKEHAM, P. (1978), 'An Approach to Financing Training — 'Compensatory Funding', Bulletin of Economic Research, 30, 2, November.

MANPOWER SERVICES COMMISSION (1982), Corporate Plan 1982-1986, April.

MARRIS, R. (1964), The Economic Theory of Managerial Capitalism, Macmillan.

MARSHALL, Alfred (1920), Principles of Economics, 8th edition, reprinted 1962, Macmillan, London.

MEE, G. and WILTSHIRE, H. (1978), Structure and Performance in Adult Education, Longman, London.

MERRITT, G. (1982), World Out of Work, Collins, London.

METCALF, D. and RICHARDSON, R. (1980), 'Labour' in A.R. Prest and D.J. Coppock (eds.) The UK Economy, 8th edition, Weidenfeld and Nicolson, London.

MINCER, J. (1962), 'On-the-job Training: Costs, Returns, and Some Implications', Journal of Political Economy, LXX, 5, 2, Supplement, October.

MICHAELSON, Jacob, B. (1978), 'Financing Lifelong Learning: The Case Against Institutional Grants', School Review, 86, 3, May

MINER, J. (1963), Social and Economic Factors in Spending for Public Education, Syracuse University Press, Syracuse.

MUELLER, D.C. (1979), Public Choice, Cambridge University Press.

MUSHKIN, Selma, J. (1972) (ed.) Public Prices for Public Products, The Urban Institute, Washington.

NATIONAL INSTITUTE FOR ADULT EDUCATION (1970), Adequacy of Provision, Leicester.

NG, Yew-Kwang (1972), 'Value Judgments and Economists' Role in Policy Recommendation', Economic Journal, 82, 327, September.

NISKANEN, W. (1971), Bureaucracy and Representative Government, Aldine-Atherton, Chicago.

OAKESHOTT, Robert, (1978), 'Industrial Co-operatives: The Middle Way', Lloyds Bank Review, 127, January.

OATEY, M. (1970), 'The economics of training with respect to the firm', British Journal of Industrial Relations, 8, 1.

ORGANISATION FOR ECONOMIC CO-OPERATION AND DEVELOP-MENT, (1975), Education, Inequality and Life Chances, Paris.

ORGANISATION FOR ECONOMIC CO-OPERATION AND DEVELOP-MENT, (1977), Learning Opportunities for Adults: Participation in Adult Education, Volume IV, Paris.

PEACOCK, A., GLENNERSTER, H. and LAVERS, R. (1968), Educational Finance: Its Sources and Uses in the United Kingdom, Oliver and Boyd, Edinburgh.

PESTON, M. (1972), Public Goods and the Public Sector, Macmillan, London.

PESTON, M. (1979), 'Recurrent education: tackling the financial implications' in T. Schuller and J. Megarry (eds.) Recurrent Education and Lifelong Learning, Kegan Page, London.

PESTON, M. (1981), 'The finance of recurrent education: some theoretical considerations' in Public Choice, 36, 3.

PETTMAN, B.O. (1973), (ed.), Training and Retraining, Transcripta Books, London.

POND, Chris (1982), 'Taxation and Public Expenditure' in A. Walker (ed.) Public Expenditure and Social Policy, Heinemann Educational Books, London.

PREST, A.R. (1975), Public Finance in Theory and Practice, Weidenfeld and Nicolson, London, 5th edition.

PREST, A.R. (1982), 'On Charging for Local Government Services', Three Banks Review, March.

PSACHAROPOULOS, G. (1977), 'The Perverse Effects of Public Subsidisation of Education or How Equitable is Free Education?', Comparative Education Review, 21, 1, February.

REIMER, Everett (1971), School is Dead, Penguin Books, London.

RIVLIN, Alice, M. (1975), 'Income Distribution — Can Economists Help?' American Economic Review Papers and Proceedings, May.

ROWLEY, C.K. (1969), 'The Political Economy of British Education', Scottish Journal of Political Economy, June.

ROYAL ARSENAL CO-OPERATIVE SOCIETY LTD. (1979), Mondragon: The Basque Co-operatives, London.

ROYAL COLLEGE OF SURGEONS OF ENGLAND (undated), Into the Eighties.

RUSSELL REPORT (1973), Adult Education: A Plan for Development, Her Majesty's Stationery Office, London.

RYAN, P. (1980), 'The Costs of Job Training for a Transferable Skill', British Journal of Industrial Relations, XVIII, 3, November.

SASSOON, J. (1982), 'Studying outside the red brick wall', The Times Higher Education Supplement, September 17.

SCHULLER, T. and MEGARRY, J. (1979), (eds.), Recurrent Education and Lifelong Learning, Kogan Page, London

SCHULTZ, T.W. (1972), (ed.), Investment in Education: The Equity-Efficiency Quandary, University of Chicago Press, Chicago.

SCHULTZ, T.W. (1974), (ed.), The Economics of the Family: Marriage, Children and Human Capital, University of Chicago Press, Chicago.

SELDON, A. (1977), Charge, Temple Smith, London.

SOCIAL TRENDS No.12, 1982 Edition, HMSO, London.

SOWELL, T. (1980), Knowledge and Decisions, Basic Books.

STOIKOV, V. (1975), The Economics of Recurrent Education and Training, International Labour Office, Geneva.

STROMSDORFER, E.W. (1979), 'Information Issues in Department of Labor Program Evaluation', in Farrell E. Block (ed.) Evaluating Manpower Training Programs, JAI Press Inc.

THOMAS, Alan, M. (1981), 'The Information Factor' in Learning Opportunities for Adults, Volume V: Widening Access for the Disadvantaged, Organisation for Economic Co-operation and Development, Paris.

THOMAS, B., MOXHAM, J. and JONES, J.A.G. (1969), 'A Cost-Benefit Analysis of Industrial Training', British Journal of Industrial Relations. July.

THUROW, L.C. (1982), 'The Failure of Education as an Economic Strategy', American Economic Review Papers and Proceedings, May.

TOUGH, A. (1971), The Adult's Learning Projects, Ontario Institute for Studies in Education, Toronto.

TOUGH, A. (1978), 'Major learning efforts: recent research and future directions', Adult Education, 28, 4.

TOWNSEND, P. (1979), Poverty in the United Kingdom, Allen Lane, London.

UNILEVER (1982), Unilever Report and Accounts 1981, London.

VAIZEY, J. et al. (1972), The Political Economy of Education, Duckworth, London.

VINCENT, J. (1980), 'France' in Comparative Study of the financial, legislative and regulatory structure of vocational training in the Federal Republic of Germany, France, Italy, the United Kingdom, European Centre for the Development of Vocational Training, Berlin.

VINOKUR, A. (1980), 'Economic Analysis of Lifelong Education' in R.H. Dave (ed.) Foundations of Lifelong Education, Unesco Institute of Education/Pergamon Press.

WEISBROD, B.A. (1964), External Benefits of Public Education: An Economic Analysis, Princeton University Press.

WEISBROD, B.A. (1977), The Voluntary Nonprofit Sector, Lexington Books, Lexington, Mass.

WEST, E.G. (1981), 'Comment on H. Glennester' in Public Choice, 36, 3.

WILES, P. (1974), 'The correlation between education and earnings: the External-Test-Not-Content Hypothesis (ETNC)', Higher Education, February.

WILLIAMS, A. (1974), 'Need' as a demand concept (with special reference to health)' in A.J. Culyer (ed.), Economic Policies and Social Goals: Aspects of Public Choice, Martin Robertson, London.

WILLIAMS, G. and WOODHALL, M. (1979), Independent Further Education, Policy Studies Institute, London.

WILLIAMSON, O.E. (1964), The Economics of Discretionary Behaviour: Business Objectives in the Theory of the Firm, Prentice Hall.

WINTERHAGER, W.D. (1980), 'The Federal Republic of Germany' in Comparative study of the financial, legislative and regulatory structure of vocational training in the Federal Republic of Germany, France, Italy and the United Kingdom, European Centre for the Development of Vocational Training, Berlin.

WOODHALL, M. (1977), 'United Kingdom Adult Education and Training: An Estimate of the Volume and Costs' in Learning Opportunities for Adults, Volume IV, Organisation for Economic Co-operation and Development, Paris.

WOODHALL, M. (1980), The Scope and Costs of the Education and Training of Adults in Britain: Developments in the Seventies, Occasional Paper Four, Advisory Council for Adult and Continuing Education, Leicester.

WOODHALL, M. (1982), Student Loans: Lessons from Recent International Experience, Policy Studies Institute, London.

ZIDERMAN, A. (1978), Manpower Training: Theory and Policy, Macmillan.